MW00390502

Twice Blessed

Also by Kathryn Tucker Windham

Treasured Alabama Recipes

13 Alabama Ghosts and Jeffrey

Exploring Alabama

Jeffrey Introduces 13 More Southern Ghosts

Treasured Tennessee Recipes

Thirteen Georgia Ghosts and Jeffrey

Treasured Georgia Recipes

13 Mississippi Ghosts and Jeffrey

Alabama, One Big Front Porch

Thirteen Tennessee Ghosts and Jeffrey

Southern Cooking to Remember

The Ghost in the Sloss Furnaces

Count Those Buzzards! Stamp Those Grey Mules!

Jeffrey's Latest 13: More Southern Ghosts

A Serigamy of Stories

Odd -Egg Editor

My Name is Julia

A Sampling of Selma Stories

TWICE BLESSED

Kathryn Tucker Windham

with photographs by the author

The Black Belt Press

Montgomery

Black Belt Press

P.O. Box 551

Montgomery, AL 36101

ISBN 1-881320-47-2

The Black Belt, defined by its dark, rich soil, stretches across central Alabama. It was the heart of the cotton belt. It was and is a place of great beauty, of extreme wealth and grinding poverty, of pain and joy. Here we take our stand, listening to the past, looking to the future.

For Dr. Rhoda Coleman Ellison,
my English teacher at Huntingdon College,
who guided me into writing
about people and places I know and love

CONTENTS

Preface

When I was growing up, I used to hear old people say, "Well, it's time I got my worldly house in order," and I wondered what they meant. Now I know. As I move into my late seventies, I am caught up by a sense of urgency to get my life and my possessions organized, to curtail my activities and to toss away clutter so that I can free myself to savor the remaining days God gives me.

But before I become totally involved in filling boxes with books for the library, gathering up clothes for the Salvation Army, and disposing of letters and photographs (the most difficult task of all), I want to leave some record of my happy life.

My two grandsons (I was nearly seventy before I had a grandchild) are too young to remember the active years of the grandmother they both call Ghost, the years when my energy matched my widespread interests. I want them to know about the work and pleasures, so often intertwined, that claimed my time and attention. I want to tell them about the experiences that have made me laugh and, yes, the experiences that made me sad, though I will not dwell on the latter.

Looking back, I know that my greatest blessings have been my loving family and my stimulating friends. My life has also been enlivened by a curiosity that has lured me into unexpected adventures, taunted me to experiment with latent talents, and guided me into an awareness of the wonders each day brings.

And through all my years, happiness, like a cloud of applauding angels, has accompanied me and urged me on.

Twice Blessed

GEES BEND

Gee's Bend

"Gee's Bend? Ain't no way to miss it." My informant rose from the bench outside a country store near Selma and walked over to my car. "You just go to Alberta," he said, pointing down the blacktop highway, "then turn left and keep the straight road. When you can't go no more, you're in Gee's Bend. Ain't no way to miss it," he repeated. "But I don't know why you want to go there."

I wasn't sure why I wanted to go either. Perhaps it was my newspaper reporter's curiosity that prompted the trip. I had heard stories about Gee's Bend for years, and I felt it was time for me to go see for myself what that isolated community in the deep loop of the Alabama River was really like.

I turned off the highway at Alberta. Soon, despite the directions I was given, I thought surely I was lost—the narrow, unpaved road seemed to go on endlessly, leading to nowhere. I met three or four pickup trucks, each trailing a plume of yellow dust. The drivers, all black men, nodded and lifted a hand in greeting as we passed. In the style of rural people everywhere, I returned their greetings.

Finally a sharp left turn took me into the community. Frame houses, each built on the same basic plan, were scattered along the main road and beside the sandy lanes. Some yards were bright with late summer flowers, others were parking lots for junk cars, their gutted remains sitting on concrete block biers shrouded with tall stalks of mullein and jimson weed.

I drove past the big, weathered store where clusters of men and teenage boys were congregated on the wide porch. Four men were perched on upended wooden drink cases around a homemade board, two watching and two playing a game of checkers with bottle tops. Two lanky youths leaning against one of the splintery posts that supported the metal roof were laughing with a friend who sat dangling his legs off the edge of the porch. After I had made a circuit of the community, I came back and took a picture of the store and its loiterers. I'm glad I did; the next time I went to Gee's Bend, the building was gone. Only the wide concrete steps–four steps leading to nothingness–marked the spot where the store had stood. And for years afterwards, until they, too, disappeared, those steps were a gathering place for idle men and boys who came there to sit and talk, as though waiting for a dilatory merchant to open for business.

The sign said BOYKIN, but everybody still calls it Gee's Bend.

One of my first pictures in Gee's Bend was of these teenagers showing off their watermelons.

I took three other pictures that day: a half-dozen youths who stopped their mule-drawn wagon and held aloft big watermelons for me to see; a group of barefooted children with long cane fishing poles on their way to the river; and quilts, their bright patches sewn in random patterns, hung across a barbed wire fence to air. Those were the first of scores of pictures I would take years later, after I became more familiar with the place and the people at Gee's Bend.

Driving home to Selma after that visit, I recalled stories I had heard about Gee's Bend. I remembered 1965 when the Rev. Dr. Martin Luther King, Jr., was in Selma and had scheduled a speech in Gee's Bend.

Hand-pieced quilts airing out on a barbed-wire fence . . . and barefooted children setting off to fish in the back-waters of the Ala-bama River. One of the original federal "project" houses is in the background.

Officials from the FBI, or maybe it was the Justice Department, in Washington, called Wilcox County Sheriff Lummie Jenkins to ask what measures he had taken to insure Dr. King's safety. The sheriff, it is reported, laughed and replied, "If he don't fall in the river and if a possum don't bite him, he'll be safer in Gee's Bend than anywhere in the world!" Many years later I heard that the mule that pulled the wagon bearing the assassinated leader's coffin through the streets of Atlanta had come from Gee's Bend.

I had heard other stories about Gee's Bend, reports of the pride, resourcefulness and deep religious beliefs of the residents in that community. Nearly all of those residents were descendants of slaves brought in to work on the rich cotton plantations in the early and mid 1800s, and most of them still bear the name of the last slave owner, Pettway. I heard, too, that strange African customs still survived in some dark corners of the settlement, that African words and phrases still slipped into their conversations. I never tracked down any of the ancient rituals nor did I ever hear any of the residents, not even the oldest ones, speak in their tribal tongues. Perhaps I arrived just a little too late.

But I did not arrive too late to hear their rich voices blend in song, or to attend the August baptizings in Foster Creek, or to hear stories of how the heirs of a Camden merchant to whom they owed money "broke us up," or to join a congregation in the solemn observance of the Lord's Supper, or to listen to firsthand accounts of how "the government up in Washington put up this house for me." Nor did I arrive too late to know and become friends with some of the older people, people who carried in their memories the history of Gee's Bend as they had experienced it and as they had heard it from their parents and grandparents. I listened as snippets and sometimes whole chapters of the Gee's Bend story were told.

It was a few years later, in the early 1970s, that I became very familiar with Gee's Bend. I had left my job as reporter for the *Selma Times-Journal* (the paper had new owners who brought in new equipment and new philosophies, and I was not sure I could adjust to either) and was working as community relations coordinator for the Alabama-Tombigbee Rivers Regional Planning and Development Commission's Area Agency on Aging. Our headquarters were in Camden, the county seat of and the only real town in Wilcox County, which adjoins Dallas County where I live.

My duties included promoting Meals For the Elderly, a community-based program designed to provide a nutritious midday meal, recreation and useful information for participants in a congregate setting. One of our proposed meal sites was in Gee's Bend.

To digress a bit—as storytellers are prone to do—I remember an occasion when Washington sent a woman down to evaluate our programs, to make certain we were following the federal guidelines. I was assigned to drive her around the rural areas (ten southwest Alabama counties) we served and make her aware of the outstanding work we were doing.

I familiarized myself with all the bureaucratic language then in vogue so that I could duly impress our visitor. "Viable" was the big word at the time. I was never sure what it meant, though I was certain that unless a project was viable, no funding would come from Washington. "Parameter" was another much-used word, also vague in meaning to me, but I used those two words often as I extolled the virtues of our programs. "At this point in time" was also a highly regarded phrase, but I never could bring myself to use it. "Now" is such a satisfactory word.

There were a good many gray mules in roadside pastures along our route, and as I drove and talked, I stamped each one for good luck, a superstition carried over from my childhood. For the uninitiated, gray mules are stamped by licking the right thumb, pivoting the licked thumb in the palm of the left hand, and then striking (stamping) the left palm with the right fist. I have stamped gray mules for so many years that I do it almost unconsciously.

After watching me perform this ritual several times, my guest asked, "Mrs. Windham, would you mind telling me what you are doing?" I explained the superstition to her, and for the rest of our journey, we were both happily stamping gray mules.

When she returned to her office she wrote me, "I have not seen any gray mules in Washington, but I have been stamping gray Cadillacs. Do you suppose they will bring me good luck?"

I am not sure about the effectiveness of gray Cadillacs, but I do believe those gray mules brought good luck to our Meals For the Elderly projects, especially the site in Gee's Bend.

"YOU NEED TO talk to Roman Pettway first," I was advised when I began planning a strategy for establishing a center in Gee's Bend. "Folks in the Bend listen to what he says."

So I went to see Roman. He was standing outside his store when I drove up. I introduced myself, and told him I had come to seek his support of a government project to help old people. "I hear you're the leader in this community," I told him.

Roman smiled, hooked his thumbs in his overall pockets and leaned back against a gas pump before he replied. "I'm an international man," he told me. "People come from everywhere to talk to me. My picture has been in a lot of newspapers, and I have been seen on television. I'm an international man." He made the claim matter-of-factly, without any evidence of false pride, and I accepted his evaluation.

Our conversation was interrupted by the arrival of a group of children who came to buy candy and bubble gum. Roman went inside the store to wait on them. When he returned, I commented on his young customers and asked casually, "How many children do you have?"

"I don't have the least idea," he replied. Although I was somewhat puzzled, I did not pursue the subject. Later I learned that Roman was a lifelong bachelor. I also learned that Roman had inherited his role of community leader from his father, a prosperous, by Gee's Bend standards, preacher whose name he bore, and that he retained the role by virtue of his own industriousness and business acumen.

My immediate concern was not to quiz Roman but to get his approval and support. He gave that backing, once the plan was explained to him, and suggested other community members whose approval I should seek.

And so we set up dining and recreation facilities in a white frame building shared with Tinnie Dell Pettway's day care center. If the elderly participants, some twenty to twenty-five of them, thought it strange that the government would send a specially equipped truck on a round trip of more than one hundred miles to deliver noonday meals to them, nobody said so. Most of them had been beneficiaries of government generosity before. As one of the men told me, "If God hadn't sent the government in here to help us back in Hard Times, I don't know what would have become of us. But God sent the government, and I thank Him."

Such talk sometimes gave me the uncomfortable feeling that I was acting as an agent for the Divine. It was a role I neither sought nor filled.

Federal guidelines for the program required that, in addition to the meals, recreation must be provided at each site. Meeting this requirement was more difficult than I had anticipated. I knew from my lifelong association with them that many older blacks, particularly women, considered all card-playing sinful, but I did not know that they would also put dominoes, checkers and other board games in the same category, all instruments of the devil.

"Don't bother 'bout us," the participants told me. "We'll just sing and pray a little bit." And they did. They sang the songs, some mournful and some joyful, that they had sung since childhood, and not one mouthful of food was ever eaten until it had been properly blessed. If there were government guidelines to prohibit such a service of praise and thanksgiving, I made sure not to know about them!

Occasionally they worked on crafts, making waste baskets out of pastel-colored egg cartons and such. The Home Demonstration Agent came to talk to them every now and then, and sometimes Eugene Witherspoon, his shock of hair as white as the ball of nylon cord he held, would demonstrate the skill of weaving fish nets. The worn wooden shuttle, smoothed by the brown hands that held it, flashed back and forth, repeating the same patterned motions that must have marked the making of nets beside African streams . . . how many centuries ago?

Perhaps it was Eugene's net-making artistry that put the notion in my head. I'm not sure. In any event, I decided the group at Gee's Bend might like to take art lessons. Surely drawing and painting would not be considered sinful! So I applied for a small grant from the Alabama State Council on the Arts and Humanities to fund an art program, and, much to my surprise, the application was approved. The only other grant I had ever received was one submitted, half seriously, to study black funeral customs.

Money was not all I needed: I had to find an artist who would be willing to make the long trip down into the Bend to give lessons to older people whose backgrounds were almost totally devoid of such experiences. I needed someone who not only had a knowledge of art but who

Using a wooden shuttle, Eugene Witherspoon demonstrates the ancient art of tying fish nets.

also had the patience, understanding and enthusiasm to discover and encourage the talents of fledgling artists, most of them past seventy. One day I walked into the library in Selma and saw on display a painting by Juanita Sherrod, a local black artist. I knew, even before I talked to her, that I had found my teacher.

Mrs. Sherrod, a pleasant, gracious woman, had begun to paint seriously and had studied art after she retired from years of teaching in public schools. When I went to talk to her about teaching art to elderly pupils, I waited until I had aroused her interest before I disclosed the location of the classes. Her smile slipped slowly away when I mentioned Gee's Bend. She had never been there, she told me, but she had heard many stories about the place and was not sure she wanted to go. I reassured her with accounts of the warmth and friendliness of the residents, of their deprived backgrounds and their need for the enjoyment her teaching would give them. I probably made it sound as if I were making a plea for her to go as a missionary into a foreign land. I almost was. She agreed to try.

So one morning I picked up Mrs. Sherrod and we headed toward Gee's Bend. In the car with us were rolls of white paper (a gift from Allied Paper Company in Jackson, Alabama), crayons, colored pencils, boxes of water colors, and assorted brushes, all of which I had purchased with Mrs. Sherrod's guidance. I suggested that she bring along some of her own paintings to show the class. We had many plans and ideas to discuss, and conversation was easy during the early part of our drive. After we left the main highway at Alberta, turned off by the Hicks' cotton gin and headed toward the river, conversation slowed. I could feel my passenger's apprehension growing. "How much further is it?" she asked several times. She was truly making a journey of faith.

Once we arrived, once she met her students, all uneasiness vanished. Soon we were all laughing together, spreading out the paper on the long tables, distributing the brushes and paints. Mrs. Sherrod gave her students very little instruction but a great deal of encouragement. "Paint whatever you want to," she told them. "Use whatever colors make you happy."

Hands that for lifetimes had picked cotton, scrubbed clothes on a rub board, pulled fodder, pieced quilts, milked cows, toted water, chopped wood, hoed ten thousand rows, shelled peas, dug potatoes, hands that were acquainted with drudgery, reached out for paint brushes. They painted hesitantly, slowly at first, uncertain how to handle this excursion into the unfamiliar realm of art. Not one of them had ever held an artist's brush before.

Gradually the tension and their self-consciousness vanished. They began to laugh, to tease each other and tease themselves as they guided paint-filled brushes across the paper. "What you call that? I can't quite make it out!" "Look here! How you like these flowers I painted? Just like the ones in my yard." Mrs. Sherrod walked from one artist to another, admiring their work, complimenting them on their use of color, encouraging them to add details.

They painted houses and trees and flowers and birds. They painted scenes they had carried around in their heads for years. "See?" one of them pointed out, "That's my house and down here by the road is my mailbox, and that's me loping down there to get my check."

Across the room, Martha Jane Pettway began to sing, "'Bird on the limb. Limb on the tree. Tree on the ground. Green grass growing all around, all around. Green grass growing all around!' I learnt that song in that little old piece of school I went to. There's more to it, but I done forgot the rest. I'm drawing it, though."

"The limb and the tree and the green grass are fine," I told Martha Jane when she showed me her picture, "but I don't see the bird."

"He flew off 'fore I could paint him," Martha Jane laughed.

A cluster of orange and purple flowers painted by See Bell Kennedy at the Meals for the Elderly site in Gee's Bend was used on the cover of the quarterly published by the Alabama Council on the Arts and Humanities. The picture was the first work of art the Gee's Bend resident had ever done.

Mrs. Sherrod was silent as we left the Bend and headed home, but it was a silence of sorting out memories, not of apprehension. "They're so sweet. So sweet," she whispered. I nodded in agreement. "What time will you pick me up next week? I'd like to go a little early . . ." So the lessons continued.

Mrs. Sherrod was proud of her pupils, as well she should have been. A patch of flowers painted by See Bell Kennedy in bright orange and purple against a swirly blue sky was used on the cover of Ala-Arts, the quarterly publication of the state arts council, and inside the magazine was an account of Mrs. Sherrod's art classes, together with the picture of the tree Martha Jane Pettway had sung about and drawn.

DURING THE FOUR years (1973–1977) I worked with the Area Agency on Aging, I visited Gee's Bend rather often, but our projects were scattered over a large area so I did not get there as frequently as I would have liked. It was only after I left the agency that I really came to know the people in Gee's Bend and the history of that place. My youngest child was out of college, I had no financial responsibilities, so I decided to earn a living with my stories, both oral and written–to be my own boss.

The combination of storytelling and writing kept me busy. Actually storytelling kept me so busy that I had little time to devote to writing but I did not mind at all. I figured that I had already put enough words on paper to fill my allotted quota, whatever that might be. My lifestyle, another word I dislike, was quite satisfactory.

Then in 1979 the Southern Women's Archives of the Birmingham Public Library received a grant from the National Endowment for the Humanities for a yearlong study to photograph the people of Gee's Bend and to record their memories on tape. Dr. Marvin Whiting, director of the Archives, offered me the interviewer's job, and I accepted immediately. I was eager to go back to Gee's Bend.

The photographer for the study was John Reese, a man about my age, from Chelsea in Shelby County, who knew nothing about Gee's Bend and had reservations about accepting the assignment. Only after he had gone down to the Bend with Dr. Whiting and me, had bought a Coca-Cola from Roman Pettway (the international man) at his store, had heard the talk and laughter of hunters swapping tales around a battered pickup truck, and had listened to the singing at the Meals for the Elderly site did he agree to become the photographer. John is a perfectionist, a sensitive man who was moved by the dignity and the God-fearing humility of his subjects. Not once in his hundreds of photographs did he fail to capture, along with a striking likeness, the touch of humor or the sly look or the deep faith that marked each character. John Reese's photographs of Gee's Bend, particularly his pictures of church services and of the August baptizings in Foster Creek, are so guileless, so tender, that I cannot look at them without emotion.

Occasionally John and I drove down to the Bend together, but more often we had separate schedules. He took his camera equipment, and I took a tape recorder, note books and pens. I have never liked to use a tape recorder or to take notes during an interview (recorders and notebooks tend to make subjects nervous and inhibited, I think) but my terms of employment required these impediments. To be truthful, I'm thankful now that I preserved the gentle, unhurried voices of my Gee's Bend friends.

Conducting the interviews was a simple pleasure, but I also needed an accurate history of Gee's Bend, the land itself and the people who had lived there. My search took me to the deed books, the marriage records, the wills recorded in the Wilcox County courthouse; to letters preserved by members of the Gee and Pettway families; to material filed in the Alabama Department of Archives and History; to a large collection of letters written by Adrian Sebastian VandeGraaff during his ownership of the land, now housed in the Alabama Collection at the University of Alabama; and to scores of government reports from the 1930s and 1940s.

Early in my research, one of the residents of Gee's Bend assured me that the original and correct name of those fertile acres was Jesus' Bend but that the name had been mispronounced and thus corrupted through the years. He believed that story completely and was deeply troubled by the name change.

Actually the place was named by and for Joseph Gee, who came from Halifax County, North Carolina, and established a plantation in the rich, remote crook of the river as early as 1816. Family tradition, undocumented but plausible, has it that Joseph Gee married an Indian princess (the most romantic version of the tale says she was a daughter of Alexander McGillivray, greatest of the Creek Indian chieftains) in Alabama and took her to North Carolina to meet his aristocratic family. Instead of being charmed by her beauty and grace, as he had expected them to be, his family members treated her with scorn. Their behavior so angered Joseph that he returned to Alabama and vowed never again to have any dealings with his kin. Joseph Gee died in late 1824 while on a business trip to Mobile to sell cotton from his plantation. The death report listed him as a bachelor. He left no will.

After a series of legal maneuvers, Charles and Sterling Gee became owners of their uncle's plantation. The estate included twelve men slaves, fourteen women slaves, ten girl slaves and eleven boy slaves, ranging in value from fifty dollars to $840 each, for a total value of $13,842.50. Charles and Sterling seem to have been poor managers or to have suffered unfortunate financial reverses; by 1845 they were heavily in debt to their Carolina kinsman, Mark H. Pettway. In November of that year they deeded all of their Gee's Bend holdings to him in settlement of a debt of twenty-nine thousand dollars.

And so the Gees departed, leaving their name on the land. In came the Pettways, who left their name on the people.

Along with his family (he had eight children), Mark Pettway brought his slaves, one hundred or more of them, who walked beside or behind the wagon train that moved the family to Gee's Bend. Though they may have borne other names on other plantations, once they reached Gee's Bend they all became Pettways. Today more than half the residents of the Bend bear that name.

The fifty-year ownership of the 3,995.5 acre plantation at Gee's Bend ended for the Pettways in January 1895 when John, son of Mark, sold the property to Duncan Dew, Jr., of Greene County, Alabama, for ten thousand dollars.

The white Pettways then left, but the black Pettways stayed. They lived in the same pole cabins where they and many of their parents and grandparents had been born. They planted, plowed, hoed, tended cattle, picked cotton, harvested vegetables and watched the seasons come and go just as they always had. The only difference in their lives was that now they paid their rents or divided their crops not with the "boss man" who lived in the big house called Sandy Hill but with a man who sometimes came by steamboat to see his property and his tenants. So it mattered not at all to them when the acres were transferred first to Joseph Dew and then to a Tuscaloosa lawyer, Adrian Sebastian VandeGraaff, whose name was harder to remember and to pronounce.

Soon after he purchased the land, VandeGraaff wrote a friend a description of the place:

> The houses are better than those I am accustomed to see in this part of the state. Some of them are ornamented with filigree work such as we see in cottages in our town, but never before in the houses

> occupied by Negroes in the country. About the houses there are gardens, nicely fenced in and containing fruit trees as well as vegetables. This too is exceptional. I was told that there are tenants on this place who have accumulated as much as a thousand dollars, and who procured their own advances or farming supplies on their independent credit in Mobile. . . .The same Negroes and their descendants are upon it who tilled it as slaves, and in much greater degree than I ever supposed it to be anywhere possible, it has preserved the features of the old plantation life.

The first year he operated the Gee's Bend plantation, VandeGraaff made over four thousand dollars, but he later suffered financial losses ("I am in a chronic state of impecuniosity," he wrote). Though he lost his mortgaged home in Tuscaloosa, he managed to hold on to Gee's Bend. At his death in 1922, one of his sons, Hargrove, took over the management of the plantation. The tenants made their lease arrangements and paid their rents to a "boy" some of them had helped raise, but everything else was just the way it had always been.

IT WAS THE Great Depression that brought change to Gee's Bend. News of the stock market crash of 1929 was slow in reaching the Bend—if it ever did reach there—just as most news from the outside world was. The nearest town, Camden, was across the river, only five miles away, but it could be reached only by a small, rickety ferry or by traveling forty miles by land to cross on the nearest bridge. Many natives of Gee's Bend grew to adulthood without ever venturing as far from home as Camden.

But even though they knew nothing of the stock market crash, its aftershocks rocked the Bend. The price of cotton, the staple they depended on, fell to five cents a pound. The years' crop did not bring enough money to pay E.O. Rentz, the Camden merchant who advanced them supplies for their farming needs, what they owed. For the first time in their lives, many Benders were in debt, and an unaccustomed feeling of uneasiness hovered over the Bend. As had always been their way, they turned to the church, to God, for solace. They gathered at the church to sing and to pray for God's help.

As if in direct answer to their prayers, Mr. Rentz agreed to hold their cotton in his warehouse until the price went up and to continue to advance them the seed and other basic supplies they needed to make another crop. He had dealt with them for years, and he knew them to be honest, hard-working people who would pay their debts, who took pride in their reputation for maintaining good credit. He did, however, take a lien on their personal property–just in case.

This arrangement continued for three years. The people in Gee's Bend had no money, but they did have land to grow food on, a river to fish in, their weathered houses for shelter and enough "furnish" from Mr. Rentz to see them through the winters and planting times.

Then in the summer of 1932 Mr. Rentz died. With him died the old way of life in the Bend.

Some sixty families, more than half the residents of Gee's Bend, were deeply in debt to Mr. Rentz. They had no estimate of how much they owed: the only records of their dealings were kept by the merchant himself, in the safe in his store. Though they expected–and dreaded–troubling times to follow the death of their longtime benefactor, they were totally unprepared for the devastation that descended on the Bend.

Elderly witnesses told me how agents of the administrator of Mr. Rentz's estate came without warning one fall day in 1932 and swept the Bend clean of their chattel. "Broke us up" is the expression they used. They told of a man on a spotted horse who crossed the river on the ferry, bringing a wagon and helpers with him. Those men, they said, hastily began gathering up everything they could find: plows, hoes, axes, chains, saws, hammers, shovels, corn, eggs, syrup, sweet potatoes, hogs, chickens, peanuts, sugar cane, dried peas—everything. They loaded the confiscated property onto wagons and carts, also confiscated, pulled by mules and horses that had spent their entire lives in Gee's Bend. Cows were herded up and driven behind the loaded wagons.

The Benders watched in helpless dismay as the long wagon train, carrying all they owned in the world, moved down the road to the ferry. They had indeed been "broke up."

It was a long, hard winter. Planting season was over, and even if it had not been, there was nothing to plant nor were there tools to plant with. People shared what little food they had. Men became expert at throwing sticks to kill fleeing rabbits, at shooting squirrels with slingshots, at grabbling fish and snaring birds. "We like to have starved, but seem like God always sent us a little something to eat. He taken care of us somehow," a survivor told me.

As always, they turned to God in their time of trouble. They sang and they prayed for deliverance. When they had nothing else to share, they shared their faith in God. "The Lord will provide," they assured each other. The Divine help they sought was slow in coming, but it did come.

The Red Cross, learning of the plight of the starving families, sent meal, flour and a few other staples across the river by boat, but it was not until 1933 that any real help came. That year one of President Franklin D. Roosevelt's relief programs provided a few jobs for men to work on the county roads three days a week at fifty cents a day. The following year another of the "alphabet agencies" provided them with the essentials to begin farming again.

During those years of poverty, Hargrove VandeGraaff, their absentee landlord, let them occupy their houses rent free, but he was almost as poor as they were so he could give them no financial assistance. Then in March 1937, Hargrove VandeGraaff sold all 7,425.74 acres of Gee's Bend to the Alabama Rural Rehabilitation Corporation for eighty-nine thousand dollars.

The biggest change since the freeing of the slaves was on its way.

Agricultural planners in President Roosevelt's administration made the development of Gee's Bend Farms a pilot project. Soon planners were laying out a model community of houses, school, commissary, gin, canning plant, clinic and church. Even the first of these visitors recognized the importance of religion in the lives of the people.

In fact, it may have been their singing of their old-time songs of faith that was responsible for bringing the New Deal project to Gee's Bend. When the plan was in its early stages in Washington, Dr. Will Alexander, director of the Farm Security Administration, came down to Alabama to meet with leaders in Montgomery, to see the land at Gee's Bend, and to talk with the people there. The community gathering at Gee's Bend was held in the frame church, and, as was their custom, the people began the meeting with a service of prayer and song.

After a bit, Dr. Alexander slipped out of the church and said to one of his assistants, "We've got to do something to help these people. These are God-fearing people. Sinners can't sing like that!" His eyes were brimming with tears.

It was Dr. Alexander, the head man himself, who expedited plans to change Gee's Bend from a community of poor tenant farmers into a cooperative of independent families living in substantial houses they would help build and would later own.

Before Dr. Alexander and his cohorts could launch their plans, they had to have the approval of Little Pettway, the community leader. The government officials would talk to the slight, balding, barefooted, very black, soft-mannered man, and if he thought their plan was all right, it would be carried out. Little Pettway and his wife, Martha Jane, set the example for their neighbors by signing up for one of the new houses the government men talked about and promised. The tree that Martha Jane drew in the Arts for the Elderly class years later may have grown in their yard. After Little's death, she continued to live in their house, and children and grandchildren moved in and out as their needs required.

The first parcel of land was bought by the Rev. Roman Pettway, Sr., according to Roman Pettway, Jr., who occupied the house built there until his death.

Whenever possible, the new houses were built on the same sites where the occupants' pole or plank houses stood. The typical house had three bedrooms, living room, dining room, kitchen with an iron cook stove (this was the first stove many Gee's Bend homemakers ever had), and a screened front porch. There was no electricity or running water, but each house had a bored well with a hand pump in the yard, and each house had a sanitary outdoor privy. Among the outbuildings were a chicken house, a large barn and a smokehouse. Construction on the ninety-seven dwellings (some accounts place the number at 101) began in September 1937, and was completed in June 1940.

During that period the government also constructed a commissary, school, clinic, gin, grist mill, and church in its model community. The new school opened in October 1938, with four teachers and 209 pupils, 105 of them in the first grade. Ages of the first-graders ranged from six to twenty-two years.

Most observers and participants agreed that the Gee's Bend cooperative project, unlike many other government-sponsored ventures, was almost totally successful.

Then in 1945 Congress ordered the Farm Security Administration to liquidate all of its cooperative farming projects. Families at Gee's Bend, who were already buying their houses and three or four acres around each dwelling, were given the opportunity to purchase the crop lands they had been renting from the government. The land was divided into one hundred units of one hundred acres each, and each unit included rich river bottom land, pasture land, upland acres, and timber. Loans for the purchases, approximately twenty-eight hundred dollars per family, were made by the Farmers Home Administration. Yearly payments on the loans were about $125 per family.

Gee's Bend's long history of tenancy ended as families became owners of the same acres their forefathers had cultivated as slaves. It was a big change.

IT WAS NOT the last big change at the Bend. In 1949 the United States Post Office Department established a post office at Gee's Bend and changed the name to Boykin, honoring U.S. Congressman Frank Boykin of Mobile. Congressman Boykin was a colorful, flamboyant politician who, as far as anybody knew, had never visited Gee's Bend. (It is reliably reported that Boykin got large appropriation bills for his district passed by inviting Yankee colleagues down to his lodge in south Alabama to hunt wild turkeys, and making sure that each guest, none of whom was familiar with wild turkeys, had a successful hunt by releasing scores of tame turkeys in the woods where they hunted.) Nevertheless, the postal guide and official documents now list the place as Boykin, but most people continue to call it Gee's Bend.

A more devastating change came to the Bend in 1962 when Congress enacted Senator Lister Hill's Rivers and Harbors Bill, which provided that a power and navigation dam be built on the Alabama River just below Gee's Bend. Backwaters from that dam flooded much of the rich bottom land, the land that had produced some of the finest cotton and the tallest corn. The owners were paid for their water-covered acres, but somehow the relatively high price the government paid did not compensate for their grief over the loss of "the best land God ever made."

Some observers lament that the lock and dam destroyed a big dream at Gee's Bend. Other pundits say the dream died long before the dam was built, that it died when residents began to buy automobiles and pickups. Their new mobility took them out of the Bend, out of the physical and emotional confines that had marked their lives, and they and the Bend were changed forever.

Learning about the history of that long-isolated place gave me the background I needed to interview the residents. Those interviews were neither scholarly nor scientific. They followed no set pattern nor were they designed to prove or disprove any theories. They were simply natural conversations with people who shared their memories about a place they knew and loved.

MONROE PETTWAY was one of the first Benders I talked with.

"Ain't nothing down here like it used to be except the everlasting word of God," he told me. It was a cold morning. Monroe had come into his brother Roman's store to get warmed by the cast-iron stove near the front of the building. Their sister, Parzie, who was running the store for Roman, walked over to the wood pile in the corner, picked up four pieces of split oak logs and took them to the stove. Balancing her load in the crook of her left arm, she opened the square door of the stove and poked the wood in, one piece at a time. Except to move out of her way, Monroe seemed unaware of the presence of his sister. As the stove began to glow from the heat of the new fuel, Monroe backed away, pushed a black and white cat off a sack of shorts (pig feed) and settled himself on the pile.

"Some of us more slack-minded than folks used to be," he commented. "People ain't bringing up children right. That's why so many people going to jail, going to jail every hour of the day."

He shoved the cat aside again and began talking of the work he did as a child. "I was 'bout seven years old when I went to the field; went in hoeing with my oldest brother." They went to the field before breakfast and stayed 'til dark, he recalled, and somebody brought their meals to them. At dark they went home, tended to the pigs and other animals, ate supper, and spread a pallet down to sleep on.

"Seem like when Daddy get up and hit the floor, I hear him in my sleep, and I hop up. He call my name, and I say, 'Sir!' and I be ready to go," Monroe continued.

Parzie interrupted, "Daddy come through the room saying, 'Yup! Yup!!' and you hear little feetses hitting the floor."

Monroe ignored the interruption. He settled down on the sacks and talked of snakes, of singing, of hunting and cooking coons, of catching eels and finally of an early memory of Hargrove VandeGraaff.

"One day when we were little children playing in the road in the shade, he rode by on his big horse. We were too young to work, so we were out there while our parents were in the field. Hargrove reach in his pocket and he come out with a whole lot of change money and throwed it out there in the midst of us. We commenced scratching just like chickens, sifting that sand. I can't forget that!"

Monroe recalled also that "over Christmas, Hargrove would call all the men up to the big house where he would stand in an upstairs window and throw change money down to them, and they just grab and grab."

Monroe was perhaps too young to remember, but there are elderly people who recollect that sometimes, late at night, Hargrove would ride his horse naked across the pastures and down the trails that led to the river, making circuit after circuit of the Bend, his white nakedness shining like a ghost. And after his wild ride, they say he would fling himself face down on a freshly plowed furrow and lie there clutching the rich earth and sobbing until the first singing of the birds.

Still laughing at his stories about Hargrove and his change money, Monroe stood up and stretched. "Got to go fix my fence," he said. "My cows done got out." He paused to warm his hands before going out into the cold. "God has blessed me," he said. "I got health and I got understanding and I got healthy children. And I've got enough to share. I believe the Bible when it say it's better to give than to receive. I never miss what I give to the church." He paused. "I wouldn't take nothing for my journey. I want to be young, but the journey I done come I wouldn't take young for it." He walked out of the store and slammed the heavy door behind him.

Every now and then Monroe's words come back to me. I wonder about my own journey and if I would exchange it to be young again.

It was Parzie who talked to me about the drudgery of her growing up years. "My childhood ended soon, that it did!" she said. Her childhood ended when her mother died and Parzie, not yet in her teens, had to do all the housework for her father, five brothers and younger sister in addition to working in the field. "I'd work in the field until Saturday and then come home and wash the boys' overalls and fix my Daddy's shirt and clothes so he could go preach Sunday. His clothes had to look just right."

While she was working so hard, Parzie dreamed of becoming a midwife like her Aunt Louella Pettway. She begged her aunt to let her go with her to deliver babies, but her aunt refused, saying Parzie was too young. "Then after my aunt died," Parzie said, "she come to me in my rest and told me, 'You can go now.' Told me three times."

With the blessings of her dead aunt, Parzie did become a midwife and delivered more than two hundred babies. "I always prayed when I went to a patient. If anything was going to be a little different or a little odd, I would see it in my rest. See it just as good. I praised the Lord for that." She also praised the Lord for sending her to midwives' meetings in Camden and for sending her to Tuskegee Institute twice. "Oh, I enjoyed that! Stayed about a week in class.

"When I'd go out on a case, I'd take my midwife bag with me: scissors, scales, soap, towel, brush to clean my nails, pencil to do bedside writing, flashlight and eye drops. They got my records over in Camden, kept one of my bedside books there," she said proudly.

She stopped her conversation to accept payment from a customer for a Baby Ruth, cheese and crackers. The customer, the postmaster from across the road, put the cheese on a piece of heavy paper, melted it on the stove and dipped the crackers in it. "Good!" she announced as she ate the last of her snack and headed back to the post office. "Got to get back to work now."

Roman built the concrete block post office and leased it to the government. Its location, right across from his store, was good for business. At mid-morning when residents congregate to await the arrival of the mail, the road is bordered with automobiles and pickups, and the store is crowded with customers.

"About my babies," Parzie continued. "Some folks tried to discourage me from being a midwife, said I shouldn't be one because I ain't never had no baby. I told them doctors ain't had babies either.

"Now some of my babies were born with what you call veils, like cellophane bags over their heads. You keep that veil until the baby about a year old, get up where he can walk, give it to him and let him go out and lose it, and he won't see haints. They say babies born with veils can see things." She may have had more to say on the subject of veils, but the Coca-Cola man arrived to service her vending machine.

When she came back to me (I was leaning against the curved top of a wooden tool chest made slick by many years of being sat upon), she said, "Out of all my babies, not a one was named for me. I named lots of them, but not for me. Parzie. My father named me. Don't know where he got that name. One midwife had so many babies named for her—Sophie. Lord! Never heard of so many children named Sophie!" She walked over to poke up the fire.

"Can't help with birthing babies no more. State made us midwives quit. Welfare pays for all that now. It's changed—just like everything else. I still got my midwife bag, though."

A bunch of customers, most of them waiting for their mail to be put up across the street, crowded into the store as I left.

CLINTON O. PETTWAY was salvaging fish hooks from a tangle of old nets and lines at a landing on the backwaters of the Alabama River when I stopped to talk to him.

"I'm fifty-eight years old," he told me, "and been here all my life. Named Pettway now, but my family had another name in Carolina. Johnson. Was named Johnson." As he talked, he cut the rusty hooks loose with his pocket knife and laid them in a pile on the ground beside him. "When old man Pettway bought my great-grandmother in Carolina, her name was Johnson."

Still busy with his hooks, he told the handed-down story of his great-grandmother and her baby boy, Saul, who would become Clinton's grandfather.

It seems that soon after Mark Pettway became the owner of Gee's Bend, he made preparations to move his large family and their possessions, including his slaves, from North Carolina to Alabama, a long and hard journey. When he learned that one of his slave women had a new baby, he ordered her to leave the child behind.

"But you know how women is about their babies," Clinton said. "She couldn't go off and leave him. So she sewed Saul, her baby, up in a mattress ticking and put that mattress in a wagon and brought him on down here. That was my grandfather. Lived to be one hundred twenty years old. Didn't join the church until he was over one hundred. Kept a sound, settled mind, too." As he talked, he shifted a matchstick from the side of his mouth to the front and back again, back and forth very slowly.

Mention of joining the church reminded Clinton that he had made a contract with the Lord that if God would get him out of the hospital and get him better, he would go carry His word.

"I knowed I had to preach," he said, "but I was doing everything I could to miss it. Jonah and me are alike. He ended up in the whale and me in the hospital. I ain't started preaching yet, but I got to. Preaching is one of the worstest things that have to be done. I ain't saw a preacher yet that wanted to preach. It ain't what he wanted to do, it's what he got to do."

He was silent for a moment as he gathered up his fishhooks and put them in a box in his boat. He looked out across the river. Then, almost as if he were practicing a sermon, he began to speak. "Everybody in the world got a right to the Tree of Life. Two commandments will get you to Heaven: love the Lord thy God with all thy heart and might and strength; and do unto others as you would have them do unto you. That's the hardest thing to do. We ain't exactly doing that." Clinton was silent so long I thought our conversation had ended. Then he looked up at me and spoke again. "I had a vision when I was a teenager and got religion," he said.

It has long been the rule at the Pleasant Grove Baptist Church in Gee's Bend that no one could become a member until he or she seriously seeks the salvation of his or her soul. If the seeking is successful, God sends the seeker a vision. The vision must be described to the preacher and deacons, and if they believe it to be a true vision from God the person becomes a candidate for baptism. The seeker goes off alone, usually into the woods, to pray and to meditate. Sometimes the seeking lasts for weeks before the prayed-for vision comes. While I was in Gee's Bend, I heard accounts of several visions but none more vivid than the one Clinton told that afternoon at the boat landing. Two johnboats, one half-submerged, were tied in the sandy shallows, and the current lapping against their metal sides beat a soft cadence for Clinton's story.

He saw himself, he said, in a refrigerated ice house with all the doors shut and no way out. The huge blocks of ice began moving, coming together. He heard men hollering as the ice closed in on them. He prayed hard, and a door opened. As he continued to pray, other doors opened for him. When he got out, two policemen began to chase him and to shoot at him. Clinton started catching the bullets, each one about the size of a golf ball, in his hand and dropping them. He kept praying. God enabled him to jump up and fly over the policemen. Those same two policemen got a helicopter and began chasing Clinton in it. He kept flying and praying. God sent a big wind that blew rusty cups and buckets at the helicopter, and then came heavy black smoke between Clinton and the helicopter so that his pursuers could no longer see him. He came down from the sky and lit right at the church door.

Clinton was emotionally moved by the telling of his vision, an account he must have told dozens of times before. He waited to regain his composure. Then he said softly, "After God showed me that vision, I knowed I didn't have to cross Hell on a spider web."

I HEARD AN account of another vision from Indiana Pettway, who talked to me on a wide range of subjects, from to local funeral customs to growing up in a household of twelve children.

"I went to the field when I was six years old," she told me, "because I wouldn't take care of babies. No matter how Mama whupped me, I wouldn't take care of babies. So Papa took me to the field with him and set me in the shade. I was his pet. Reckon I was about eight years old when I really went to working."

Once that working started, there was scant relief from drudgery and poverty.

"Have made a whole week with boiled peas and salt. Nothing else. Didn't have shoes. Had one dress. Would wash it, dry it, iron it and put it back on. The same with my children. It was tough. Used to wash fertilizer sacks and make underskirts and boys' shirts. It wasn't worrisome to me; I wasn't used to nothing else."

She told of the death of her mother. "Mama went to church and shouted all over that church. Next day she told me, 'Indiana, I'm gonna steal away from you all.' I didn't want to believe her, but it was true." A funeral home in Camden conducted her mother's funeral, but Indiana recalled the times, back before funeral homes, when members of the local burial societies handled all the arrangements for a funeral.

"One was the Home Society," she said, "and you paid three dollars to join. Then you paid a dollar every month. When a member died, the Society would build a plank coffin and line it with black cloth. The deacons at the church would tell the brothers to dig the grave. They'd put the coffin in a wagon, and a mule would pull it, creeping along with folks walking behind."

The talk of funerals led to a discussion of church services and of visions.

"I was about seventeen years old when I had my vision," Indiana said. "Sometimes I'd walk down in the swamp to pray, and sometimes

I'd get a praying ground close to home. I saw a casket down there close to the school. I looked in the casket and Indiana was in there. I said, 'Huh! There Indiana in casket and here Indiana standing over casket.' When I said that, a lady rose up in a long white gown. Then I see myself going around a curve and found some big plums. The woman said, 'Hell hounds gonna get on your track.' Spotted hounds got after me.

"The next time I see myself, I'm trying to climb a tall mountain. Everything I catch hold to, it pull up by the roots. I scuffled and scuffled until I got on top of mountain. See myself again, I'm down in a well. I dig and dig until I hit rock. When I hit rock, water came pouring out. I was so happy! The world looked brand new. My hands looked brand new. I felt good. I couldn't never finish telling it. I'm yet telling it. It changed my whole life."

Indiana looked at me a long time, making sure I understood what she had told me.

IT WAS A GENTLER vision that Mattie Ross told me about. She was working on a brightly colored log cabin quilt while we talked.

"When I was seeking my soul's salvation, I prayed hard," she said. "I asked God to forgive my many sins and free my soul from Hell. When you get twelve years old, your sins fall on you. Until then your sins are on your parents. I prayed hard. Prayed hard. Got me a praying ground. Looked up and saw some clouds. Told God if soul was saved to make clouds go away. They did. But one mind said they was gonna do that anyhow. So I asked again if soul was saved from Hell to let a big spot of clouds disappear. They did; just went to nothing. I said, 'Thank you, Jesus!' I was so happy. I got religion that year. I love my religion."

While she sewed, Mattie talked about life in the Bend before the "project" came. She was married then to Clint O. Pettway (now deceased and not to be confused with the present Clinton Pettway) who is said to have been the strongest man, to have had the biggest feet, and to have been blessed with the most magnificent singing voice in Gee's Bend.

They lived, she said, in a one-room house made of pine poles with gashes in the ends of the poles to hold them together. The fireplace and chimney were made of sticks and mud, and the plank floor had cracks big enough to put fingers through. The wind came up through those cracks on cold nights. They slept in that one room, cooked in that room, ate in that room, and when Clint O. came from ginning their cotton, the cotton seeds were piled up in one corner of that room until planting time.

"I never thought I'd live in one of the houses them Washington men came down here and talked about," Mattie said, "but what they said was true, has come to pass. I thanked God, and I still thank Him. God gave us everything we could use—new house, smokehouse, chicken house, toilet, barn.

"I remember when we moved into our new house," she continued. "I said, 'Us going in our new house clean!' Two children—not mine—living with us then. We took us a bath. Washed up everything, mattresses and beds, scrubbed them. I didn't want my new house nasty.

"I think back to years ago when I was seeking my soul. I didn't understand God's plan then. Now I know God has work for us to do. When God converted me, he didn't convert me with no coward spirit. Sho' didn't. I stand up for Him and speak up for Him wherever I go."

I listened to her simple declaration of faith, and I wished that I believed as deeply as she does; that I, too, had sought long enough and prayerfully enough to be blessed with a life-changing vision.

IF MY FRIEND Arie Pettway had a vision, we never discussed it. Arie died in the early summer of 1993, two weeks before I returned to Gee's

Bend for a long-promised and too-long postponed visit. She died, her kinfolks told me, of injuries suffered in a fall at her home.

When I first met her, Arie was recovering from injuries received in two separate accidents, an automobile wreck that had "buggered up" her hip and a fall over a stump while trying to beat a bad dog off a hog. Her arm, shoulder and hand had been broken in the fall, but they had healed. She was sitting on her front porch, her foot propped up on a boot jack, and was eating watermelon with her grandchildren when we met.

"If my hip wasn't broke, I could grab a watermelon under each arm and run away," she said. "When I was young, I seen times I went through a fellow's watermelon patch and grab two watermelons and whoosh–!" She laughed, took a bite of melon and spit the seeds out in the yard. She wiped her hands on her dress, picked up her walking stick and invited me in to see some of her quilts.

Arie led the way through the front door to a hallway that connected a house trailer at an awkward angle. She pulled bright-colored quilts out of cabinets where stacks of her handiwork had been shoved, and, with the help of a grandson conscripted for the duty, she spread them out on several unmade beds. I had never seen any of the patterns before.

"Who taught you to quilt?" I asked. I asked, too, where the unusual patterns came from.

"Nobody taught me to quilt. My sister and our first cousin and I would get together and get rags to sew, to practice on. My daddy worked across the river in the white folks' yard, and he would bring home newspapers to paper the house for Christmas. Us would see puzzles and things in the paper and cut the cloth like them. Made our own patterns. Named them what us wanted to: Hand and Wrist, Finger Five, Nine Patch, all like that. Learned to make pretty quilts."

Arie Pettway not only created unusual quilts, she could also play the accordion she inherited from her father.

Arie eased herself down onto the side of a bed and talked about how she and her sister would hang around older quilters, married ladies, who didn't mind taking up time with them. One of those was Cousin Fancy who "if she ain't one hundred is snatching it!" She talked about how the neighbors would gather to help quilt, so many that somebody would have to go get more chairs for them to sit in.

"Whatever needed doing, we did," she said. "If somebody needed a whupping, we whupped them. If somebody wanted to eat dinner, we cooked. I had a sister could cook so good the angels might heist their singing when she set the table!" She chuckled and wiped her mouth as though savoring the recollection of her sister's cooking.

Arie never talked to me about her religion, but I did hear her speak in church one November Sunday during a long worship service. The congregation had dedicated a song to Sister Kathryn, "O, Let-a Me Ride." I had heard it sung during the baptism at Foster Creek in August,

> I been converted, O, let-a me ride.
> I got my ticket, O, let-a me ride.
> I'm going to Heaven, O, let-a me ride.

with the refrain repeated again and again. A deacon had ended his prayer, prayed against a background of song and moaning, with a plaintive plea, "Lord, catch my little soul and save it up in yo' kingdom." Sister Nettie Kennedy had stirred the emotions of the congregation with her singing of "Heavy Load."

Arie, leaning on her stick, rose from her place in the church and began to speak. "I'm glad to be here and listen to that good singing 'cause I love singing. I'm just sorry I done fooled around here and got old and can't sing. I'll stay here seventy-one more years if the Lord will let me."

She laughed. "Kinda telling you all how old I is. Ought not to done that and me single! I know the Lord's laid His hands on me. I lean on the Lord, not like I'm propped on this stick: I'm leant back on the Lord."

I have two of Arie's quilts on beds in my house. One she called the President's Quilt has hundreds of small red, white and blue triangles sewed together to form a large circle on a background of navy blue in the center of the quilt. White six-pointed stars are appliqued on strips of red around the red, white and blue border. At the top is a red lion with a mane of navy blue triangles and a navy blue face with fierce features embroidered in red. At the foot is a navy blue eagle holding a red olive branch in one claw and a red arrow in the other. The red, white and blue quilt has a brown lining. "It was all the cloth I had," Arie said.

My other quilt Arie called the Tree of Life. It sings with bright colors–red, green, blue and yellow. Rising from the center is a tree trunk of muted blue and green mingled print, quilted so that you can almost feel the rough bark. Spreading out from the trunk are branches of triangular leaves, and in the top is an eight-pointed star of red and green. Around the base of the tree, Arie quilted a cotton print of flowers–hyacinths, tulips, daffodils and daisies–a garden of spring beauty. At the foot of the tree, as though he were guarding a precious treasure, is an eagle with his wings outstretched.

How blessed I am to have these reminders of Arie's artistry and of her friendship! I know God must have "caught her little soul and saved it in His kingdom."

WILLIE QUILL Pettway had on his uniform and was wearing his badge when I stopped by his house to see him. Willie Quill was the first black deputy sheriff in Wilcox County, and he was justifiably proud of that honor.

The deputy was born in Gee's Bend in 1928 and has spent all his life there, he told me. He talked about the pole house he grew up in, its inside walls ceiled with pasteboard from old boxes, and he talked about being water boy, his first job, for crews building the project houses. "Oh, they drink so much water!" he laughed.

I had met Willie Quill on one of my earlier visits to Gee's Bend, had come upon him giving lessons in firearms safety to a group of elderly residents near the church. When I walked up to the grove of pine trees where they were gathered, he was explaining the various parts of a pistol, giving special emphasis to the safety catch.

"Some of these folks got guns and don't know how to use them," he said to me. "I'm giving them lessons for their own safety." He had tacked a target up on a tree and was supervising his students while they shot at it. They were terrible shots: many of them not only missed the bull's-eye but missed the whole target and tree.

"Do you want to try?" Willie Quill asked me, and he offered me his pistol, a heavy service revolver. I really did not want to try, but if I declined, I might lose face with people whose respect I was trying to win. I faced the same prospect if I shot poorly. It had been many years since I had held a pistol in my hand, and I felt very uncomfortable. I tried to recall the instructions my older brother had given me: Don't rush. Hold steady. Sight along the barrel. Squeeze the trigger gently.

I took Willie Quill's gun and did precisely what I had been taught to do such a long time ago. The bullet smacked right in the middle of the bull's-eye! A gasp of admiration and amazement went up from the spectators. Even Willie Quill was impressed. "Want to shoot again?" he asked. I declined. I was not about to risk my reputation as a master marksman by taking a second shot.

Word spread quickly throughout the Bend: "That white woman sho' can shoot!"

Deputy Sheriff Willie Quill Pettway gives an older Gee's Bend resident instuctions on the safe use of a pistol.

Willie Quill and I laughed about that episode the afternoon I went to interview him.

He didn't laugh when he told about the afternoon a big truck drove up and backed into a ditch so helpers could load a black bull, Willie Quill's pet, into the truck. "Man said Papa owed him money, and they took my bull. Was jet black. Had long white horns. I named him Son. He could plow, plow. I loved that bull. Son. It hurted me so bad when they come and took him. I still don't believe Daddy owed that man no money."

Embarrassed by his show of emotion, he shook his head and muttered, "Long time ago. Long time ago–"

Seeking to ease the tension, I asked, "Where'd you get your name?"

The deputy chuckled and declared he's the only person he ever heard of named for a steamboat. "Doctor named me. Named me Nettie Quill for a boat used to be on the Alabama River, but my Daddy didn't like that name, said he had worked too hard on the Nettie Quill. So they changed it to Willie Quill, put that on my birth certificate: Willie Quill Pettway."

He was eager to tell about his visions that finally came after a lengthy period of seeking and praying. He told in detail about how God had sent a mourning dove and rain after a long dry spell as his signs and had raised from the dead a mule Willie Quill's father thought the youth had ridden to death. "I got to the church and I said, 'Now, Lord, if these been my signs, then I want you to lead me on the mourners' bench tonight. I'm tired of sitting up there and them people marching around me and talking, and look like I'm the only one going to Hell. So now I want you to meet me there with the Holy Spirit.' And He did!"

My interview with Willie Quill had gone well. He had provided me with background information I needed in addition to telling me some interesting stories, and I was about to leave when he told me the most touching story of all, the story of his first pair of shoes.

"I was twelve years old when I got my first pair of shoes," he began. "Up 'til then, all the time I was in school I didn't have no shoes. My sister could wear my mama's shoes, but my daddy didn't have but one pair, and he had to go to work in them. My foots was so rough!

"My daddy was working on the road, and I had to take him something to eat where he worked, 'bout two miles. Had to pass this white lady's store, Miss Bessie Harrison, on the way." One cold morning, Willie Quill recalled, when he was taking food to his daddy, Miss

Bessie called to him, "Boy, is that the way you been coming down here bringing Ed's breakfast every day, coming barefooted?"

"'Yes'm,' I told her. I was so cold. She told me to come in the store and sit down. I did. She went and got a pan of hot water and put my foots down in it. That water got in them cracks in my foots. Ooooh! Then she dried my foots off and rubbed Vaseline on them and put some socks, new socks, on me. She reached up on the shelf and got this thing and measured my foot, and then she went to looking at the boxes of shoes up on the shelf. She got a pair that just fitted—a little bit big, but I didn't care. They was shoes!

"She laced them up and tied them. I didn't say anything. When she tied the last knot, I jumped up and ran all the way home. When I got home, I couldn't tell Mama nothing. I just stood there in my new shoes. Mama said, 'Where'd you get them shoes?' and I told her Miss Bessie give them to me. 'You thank her?' Mama asked. 'You go back and tell her thank you, ma'am.'"

So Willie Quill, wearing his first pair of shoes, ran all the way back to the store to thank Miss Bessie. "I found a dime going back, and I kept the dime the longest time. Finally bought a great big cap with it," he recalled. "Got to the store and thanked Miss Bessie and asked her what my daddy owed for the shoes. She told me he didn't owe nothing, that she wasn't even going to put it on the book. Well, I didn't care nothing 'bout the price of 'em. She could have charged him a hundred dollars for what I cared. I had a pair of shoes!" He paused.

"Miss Bessie. She passed not long ago. Was over in a old folks home in Camden. I'd go to see her and stand by her and look at her, but she didn't know me. She long forgot that she give me my first shoes. I ain't." His voice quivered.

Willie Quill looked down at his highly polished, almost new shoes. "Them shoes wasn't near as big as these I got on now!" he laughed. His laughter pushed a happy but painful memory aside.

JUST AS WILLIE Quill and others never get through telling about their visions, I never get through telling about Gee's Bend, about the faith and the wisdom and the pride I found there. Memories of bits of conversation, of singing, of small happenings, even of scenes that might have come from movie sets or stage plays slice unexpectedly into my mind. I remember . . .

. . . Edgar Mooney, who ran the ferry for more than a quarter of a century, telling me, "It's the same God but another world," and warning me, "You can't put two days in one, just like you can't put but one foot in a shoe. If you try to put two feet in there, it's gonna bust. Same with days."

. . . Margaret Pettway recalling how her grandfather's early morning singing waked the whole Bend to worship and work. He welcomed the day with, "Soon, one morning, soon one morning, soon one morning I heard the angels sing. They was all around my bed, O, all around my bed, Lord, all around my bed. I heard the angels sing!"

. . . Maggie Bennett describing some lazy young folks as "so sorry they ain't fit to tote guts to the buzzards!"

. . . Tinnie Dell Pettway extolling the effectiveness of the new air-conditioning system at church: "So cold it makes you feel like a saucer of ice cream!"

So rich in stories that place is, rich with people who have lived the stories they tell. Their stories are not for the cheap exploitation of Donahue or Geraldo or Oprah but are waiting for sensitive tellers who exult in the triumphant joys of plain people whose lives have been shaped by an abiding awareness of God's presence.

Perhaps nowhere was the awareness of that presence stronger than at the August baptizings in Foster Creek.

White-robed candidates for baptism arrive at Foster Creek, long-time site of this traditional rite at Gee's Bend.

I attended my first baptizing in Gee's Bend back in 1977. It was hot and sultry, as August days often are in Alabama. A few fluffy clouds gathering along the western horizon offered hope for a cooling shower. I drove through the deserted community, swathed in a Sabbath quiet, and turned onto a narrow graveled road that led to the creek. Near the creek, cars haphazardly lined both sides of the road. I eased my car through a gap in a barbed wire fence and parked in an overgrown pasture close to a sweetgum bush and a clump of shaggy weeds growing out of a fire ant mound. Even before I turned off the motor, I could hear the singing.

I followed a trio of teenaged youths along a worn cowpath to the creek. The path bordered a bluff overlooking a bend in the creek. Spectators were standing four or five deep around the bluff's edge. "Let the white lady in," a middle-aged man, sweating in his dark suit and tie, said. "Let her get where she can see." The crowd parted promptly and pleasantly to accommodate my camera and me.

Down below us, where the ground was level and sloped into the bend of the creek, Deacon Goldsby Ross held a big black umbrella over the head of the preacher, the Reverend Isaac Perkins. Reverend Perkins, a tall, slender man, wore a long white robe over his suit (a gap at the throat showed his dark tie was precisely tied), and his head was wrapped in a white turban. He stood at the edge of the water under the shade of Deacon Ross's umbrella, surrounded by perhaps a hundred or more members of his congregation, preaching and praying and moaning in a rhythm as ancient as the ritual they celebrated. Chanting and with his face lifted heavenward, he waded slowly into the still waters of the almost-stagnant creek.

Deacon Ross protected his pastor with the shade of the umbrella as long as he could reach without getting his feet wet. Then he slowly folded it and took his place on the creek bank. Other deacons, younger and stronger, followed their pastor into the water. Ahead of them waded a man with a long, stout stick to measure the depth of the water and to test the smoothness of the creek bottom.

The candidates for baptism walked one by one down a path, below and across from where I was standing, each wearing a long white robe and a white head covering. Waiting hands guided each candidate down to the creek and out to where the preacher and his helpers stood in the chest-deep water.

Along the banks, the singing, chanting and humming never ceased. It swelled and ebbed and swelled again. When the musical background

Two rows of deacons guide each newly professed Christian out to be baptized by the Rev. Isaac Perkins in the murky waters of Foster Creek.

softened, Reverend Perkins's words came clear and strong: "In obedience to the divine commandment and in recognition of your faith, I do indeed baptize you in the name of the Father and of the Son and of the Holy Spirit." With two helpers, he immersed each candidate in the murky stream. Off to the side, the man with the stick swished it through the water with a slow, rhythmic motion.

Several deacons waited to lead each newly baptized person back to the creek bank for, without exception, they came out of the water shouting, jerking and twisting in ecstasy.

One of the candidates, an older woman, walked into the water singing. I did not recognize the tune nor could I understand the words, but I did not need to: the entire congregation was silenced by the beauty and the deep feeling of her voice. As she waded toward him, the preacher talked of how she had waited so long but how prayers had reached out and brought her home. Her own happiness at being "brought home" burst forth in her song.

When the final candidate was baptized, the crowd began to disperse, going to their cars and pickups to return to the church for a service. Two men, acting as traffic directors, unsnarled the tangle of vehicles quickly and without mishap.

Meantime, up on the bluff above the creek in the privacy of an improvised dressing room made of sheets hung between pine saplings, the women and girls changed from their wet garments into their Sunday clothes, readying their physical beings to be received into the full fellowship of the Pleasant Grove Baptist Church.

That congregation no longer baptizes in the creek. In what some members consider progress, they built a concrete baptistry beside the church. I'm grateful that I witnessed the baptizings in Foster Creek, that my own life was touched by the pure joy, the welling up of love and thanksgiving, that marked those age-old rites.

I'm grateful, too, for the forces, whatever they were, that pulled me into the community called Gee's Bend.

STORYTELLING

One late spring day in 1974, the telephone on my desk at the Area Agency on Aging rang, and when I answered, a pleasant but unfamiliar voice said, "This is Jimmy Neil Smith in Jonesborough, Tennessee. I'd like for you to come tell stories at the National Storytelling Festival in October."

"I believe you have the wrong Windham," I replied. "I'm not a storyteller. It must be my daughter, Kitti Windham, you want. She has a master's degree in drama and theater."

"No, I'm sure it's you," the voice said. "I'll send you a plane ticket if you'll come."

By then I was busy figuring out which one of my fun-loving friends was trying to trick me: Smith, Jonesborough, National Festival. Too much. So I laughed and said I'd be glad to come. And I wondered what would happen next, when the hoax would be exposed. The invitation for me to participate in a national storytelling festival became a running joke in the office and in my family. The list of suggested stories, some of them unsavory, grew as did my curiosity as to who was responsible for the prank.

The teasing and the speculation had eased off, replaced by other office interests, when my plane ticket arrived. There really was a Jimmy Neil Smith and a National Storytelling Festival in Jonesborough, Tennessee. He sent along a batch of clippings about the first festival to verify its existence. Jerry Clower had been the featured storyteller at that initial event in 1973.

SO I, STORYTELLER that I was not, flew off to Tennessee one October day to tell stories at the National Storytelling Festival. I'm still amazed at my audacity.

I was familiar with storytelling, had grown up in a large family where we all told stories, but I never knew that people would travel for miles and would pay money to listen to strangers tell stories. I was amazed to learn that storytellers were paid to tell tales at festivals, conventions and even in school classrooms. I never knew that what my family considered a pleasant pastime was an occupation.

DILCY HILLEY

Where two or three are gathered together—stories are told!

The storytelling I grew up with was relaxed, spontaneous, and natural, one of our favorite forms of entertainment. When I was a child, everybody I knew told stories. Television had not yet been invented, and I even remember quite plainly the first radio our family ever had. It was an Atwater Kent with a big, round speaker. My brother, Wilson, climbed to the top of the pecan tree in our back yard to string the aerial up high so, if atmospheric conditions were cooperative, we could listen to WSM in Nashville, WAPI in Birmingham, a Meridian station, and a ranting broadcaster out in Del Rio, Texas. The static was usually terrible, and Daddy would switch the set off in disgust. So even the acquisition of a radio did not stop our storytelling.

Mealtimes were storytelling times at our house. The whole family assembled around our long oak dining room table, the table with handcarved dragons supporting it, and we talked as we ate—not with our mouths full of food, of course. "Chew and swallow before you speak," Mother used to remind me. Conversations at breakfast and at midday dinner were curtailed by work schedules: Daddy had to get to the bank, Aunt Bet and Tabb hurried down the hill to the Post Office, and I left for school. We were a punctual family, never late anywhere. I was not tardy all the years I attended school.

One of the tales my family used to tell, embellishing it as the years passed, was of my going off to school one morning when the shingle roof of our house was ablaze. I never even looked back at the neighbors on top of our house pouring water on the flames as fast as Thurza could draw the bucketsful from our well. So fearful was I that I would be late, that I waited until I reached the schoolhouse, on a hill about a mile from home, before I paused on the steps long enough to scan the horizon. Seeing no smoke, I knew the fire was out, and I went happily into my classroom, right on time.

That was the kind of story our family liked to tell. I don't recall that

I ever heard fairy stories or tales from the classics told (we read them all) but I grew up hearing about members of our family, our relatives (the relatives my sister, Annelee, did not approve of, she always referred to as "some of Papa's kinfolks") and our neighbors, people we knew. Sometimes Daddy (the older children called him Papa) told tales of local history, of the first trains to come to Thomasville, of the fire that destroyed the business district of the town, of long ago Indian massacres, of bears that came out of the swamps and toted off squealing two-hundred-pound hogs from farmers' pens.

Other members of the family told tales, too, and so did the visitors who came to eat meals with us or to sit by the wintertime fires, or to rock on the front porch in the warm weather.

Although my childhood was filled with stories (on summer nights I would fall asleep listening to the slow, rhythmic thuds of rocking chairs on the front porch and the gentle blending of familiar voices telling stories), I was seldom a teller. Like my mother, I listened more than I told. When my children were small, I read to them almost constantly, or so it seemed, and I told a few stories, but it was their daddy who was the storyteller, captivating them with stories he made up about Wessie Witch and Miss Prunella Panther and Walter Wolf and the Bug brothers, Bo and Bucky. Oh, what exciting adventures those characters had!

Later I tried to hold–or get–the attention of a seventh-grade Sunday School class, a mixture of thirty boys and girls, not one of whom wanted to attend Sunday School, by telling them Bible stories. My telling was a complete failure. When the giggling and chatter in my class disturbed other study groups in the vicinity, I would bring about a brief but welcome quiet by saying, "Let's bow our heads in prayer." I did a heap of praying the year I taught that class.

In addition to praying, there was one activity I discovered that would keep their exuberance moderately modulated. Not a single one of my pupils, I learned, had ever played a comb. So the next Sunday I brought thirty-one combs and a roll of waxed paper to class, demonstrated the technique of covering the comb loosely with waxed paper, holding it to the lips and humming. My charges were delighted. From then on, most of every Sunday session was devoted to playing combs. We played nearly every hymn in the Methodist hymnal before the year was out. Although that class continued to have a reputation for being noisy, at least it was a joyful noise we were making.

My next venture into storytelling came under the heading of "book review." It began when the late Margaret Gillis Figh, who taught English and folklore at Huntingdon College for more than forty years, and I published a collection of traditional Alabama ghost stories, a book we titled *13 Alabama Ghosts and Jeffrey.* Actually I suppose it started in 1966 when a strange something that we call Jeffrey took up residence in our house. I can't be certain that Jeffrey is a ghost because nobody has ever seen him, nor do I know anything about his background or why he chose to move in with us. I do know that Jeffrey changed my life.

Jeffrey's antics reminded me of the ghost tales I had heard Margaret Figh tell at Huntingdon, and after a series of puzzling occurrences in our house, I went to the college to discuss them with my teacher-friend. Perhaps I really went to brag to her that I might have a ghost in my house. As we conversed about Jeffrey, we began to talk about some of Alabama's famous spirits, and we agreed it was a shame that their stories had never been collected and preserved in a book. Before the visit ended, we had decided to collaborate on such a collection.

Some months after the 1969 publication of our book, I began getting a few requests from women's study clubs, garden clubs, civic organizations and such to give a book review at their meetings. Book reviews, I have found, can be very boring, even to the reviewer, so I began telling stories from the book. My audiences liked hearing the stories, and I liked telling them, but nobody, least of all me, thought of me as a storyteller. I was just a newspaper reporter who had written a book.

So that was the extent of my storytelling experience when I was summoned to Jonesborough to appear at the National Storytelling Festival. By then I had written and my friends at Strode Publishers had published two more collections of Southern ghost tales, so I had a larger number of stories to choose from.

The festival, then in its second year, was small. We tellers sat in porch swings with our listeners clustered around us, or we gathered in the shade of maple trees, sitting on blankets spread on the grass, as we told stories and listened. I told ghost stories, told them simply, just the way that Daddy would have told them on our front porch at home.

Saturday night we told stories at an olio, a word I had never heard before, at a nearby junior high school auditorium. The place was packed, and there was applause, a mighty gratifying and reassuring sound.

The whole weekend was informal, relaxed and fun.

Only a few tellers were on the program that year, so we got to know each other, became friends. Connie Regan was there. She was a librarian who later teamed up with her cousin Barbara Freeman to leave the sedate and secure world of books and go roving around the country in a dilapidated camper telling stories wherever they found listeners. Doc McConnell, his teenaged daughter Hannah, and his brother Steamer with their old-time medicine show, and red-haired poet/musician/ teacher/storyteller Lee Pennington were there, too. Lee, with the help of his wife Joy, later launched the highly successful Corn Island Storytelling Festival in Louisville, Kentucky, his home town.

We've kept in touch through the years, all of us pioneer tellers at

Jonesborough. Connie and Barbara told stories at the first Alabama Tale-Tellin' Festival in Selma, and Doc and Lee were among our early tellers here. We all served on the Board of Directors of the National Association for the Preservation and Perpetuation of Storytelling when Jimmy Neil formally founded that organization. I was the first dues-paying member of NAPPS. Jimmy Neil did have my five-dollar check framed and hanging on the wall of his office, but it got lost a few years ago. He thinks Jeffrey purloined it.

At those early NAPPS board meetings, held in cramped quarters above a coin laundry in downtown Jonesborough, we discussed ideas for expanding the festival, selected tellers and wondered how we would pay them, and drew up a constitution and bylaws. Usually we would meet for breakfast in our upstairs headquarters (we had a lot of trouble with the plumbing in those early days). I introduced my friends to one of my mother's breakfast treats, a banana sliced in a small bowl of orange juice, and by the time I left the board some eight years later, the bananas and orange juice had become traditional fare at NAPPS-oriented breakfasts.

Every year the festival grew. Other board members and I watched with a mixture of amazement and apprehension as the crowds increased each October. People converged on the historic, picturesque and usually tranquil little Tennessee town, inundating it with their enthusiasm and their elusive quests for emotional, perhaps even spiritual, experiences that they themselves were unable to define.

I have seen the festival change from the small groups of listeners on porches, in church basements and in patches of shade to throngs of people congregating in huge circus tents pitched on half a dozen vacant lots. I have watched the tellers adjust to the requirements of these huge audiences. The human voice can no longer tell the stories unassisted, so in have come tangles of electrical cables hitched to devices that magnify

Telling stories in Selma's Live Oak Cemetery.

and distort the amazing instrument of speech.

Though accepting the changes, I resent the barriers of microphones between tellers and listeners, the video cameras, the audio consoles, the lighting panels, and the spotlights. Perhaps it is the spotlights I hate most of all. The focused glare of those lights thoughtlessly and heartlessly transforms storytellers into performers–and there is a vast difference between the two.

I believe that the intrusion of this electronic equipment sucks away the very life of storytelling, robbing it of the personal touch that has always been–and should continue to be–its joy and its strength.

When I hear young storytellers extol the wonders of voice amplification and stage lighting, I find myself wishing they could have heard my father tell stories on our front porch just one summer night.

Daddy's voice was deep and well-modulated, and his quick laughter as he told the tales underscored his enjoyment of the telling. Our porch was dark except for the light from the street lamp on the corner that filtered through the tangled screen of honeysuckle, wisteria and ivy vines that shielded it from the street. Sometimes Daddy's stories were interrupted by the arrival and passing of a train (the tracks of the Southern Railroad were only a block away), a distraction that gave him time to shift the position of his rocking chair and relight his pipe. As soon as the locomotive with its noisy whistle had pulled the clacking cars out of earshot, past the Double Deck and on toward Finlay's Crossing, Daddy would pick up the story just where he left off.

I wonder what he would have thought about the trappings of modern storytelling.

In addition to the taint of show business that marks much of today's storytelling, it concerns me that the art is being too closely analyzed by scholars. I first became aware of the trend when people associated with NAPPS began asking, quite earnestly, "Is that teller a traditionalist or a revivalist?" Long and heated discussions, liberally sprinkled with references to scholarly research and recurrent thematic elements, often followed. The question, it seems to me, should be, "Is he a good storyteller?"

Yet, despite my disapproval of the use of sound equipment and of spotlights, despite my discomfort with the scholarly dissection of stories, despite my nostalgia for simpler times (this may be a serious symptom of Old Age Syndrome), I like storytelling, like to hear stories and like to tell them, and I am convinced that the gentle art of storytelling will survive.

One of the main reasons I enjoy telling stories is that it gives me instant gratification. In contrast, it will be many months between the time I put my thoughts on paper and the time they are published, and more months before they reach bookstores and libraries. That's a long time to wait for a response from readers. And when I write, even as I am writing now, I wonder if anybody will ever read my words, if what I have written will stir memories or encourage new ideas.

For years I visited schools, telling stories to children in the fourth grade and older (little children intimidate me). I miss those visits to schools, miss the pleasure of watching the expressions on young faces as the pupils become interested and involved in the story. Then when my story ended, if the children sat silent for a moment, pondering the words they had heard, I knew I had told the story well. And if, as occasionally happened, a child said, "You made me see pictures in my head," I could not wish for a higher accolade.

I do not spend days at schools telling tales anymore. As my energy level declined, the requests for me to visit classrooms increased. If I had accepted all the invitations, there would have been little time left for me to stay at home, to do any writing, to indulge in my hobbies or to be with my family (my two grandsons are growing up so fast!) and friends. Since I could not go to all the schools that invited me and since I could not decide which ones to visit and which ones to decline, I simply stopped going to any classrooms.

I miss being with the children. They and I shared a delight in the antics of Jeffrey, and we wondered if he really could be a ghost. We cavorted together along that fragile line between fantasy and fact.

I never told ghost stories to my young audiences without first telling them, "You do not have to believe in ghosts to enjoy a good ghost story. A good ghost story will stretch your imagination, make you ask if it really did happen, and if it really could be true." And I never ended a session without assuring my young listeners that, according to Southern folklore, they would never be afraid of anything and nothing bad would ever happen to them if they put their shoes under the side of their bed at night with one shoe's toe pointing under the bed and the other toe pointing in the opposite direction. Then we would laugh together. I like to end my sessions with laughter.

We understood each other, my school children and I. Sometimes parents did not understand. Occasionally I got angry letters saying, "You are going to Hell for telling ghost stories to children," and every now and then parents would forbid a few pupils to listen to my stories, claiming that I dealt in the occult. I don't believe a single one of those dissenting parents had ever heard me tell a story.

I have not lost touch with my youthful audiences entirely. They come each October to hear me tell stories in Birmingham at the Sloss Furnaces (some of them definitely feel the ghostly presence of Theopholis Calvin Jowers, a foundryman who fell to a fiery death in a furnace a century ago), at Old Alabama Town in Montgomery, at the Kentuck Festival in Northport, at the Alabama Tale-Tellin' Festival in Selma in October, at City Stages in Birmingham, at Cahaba Day and at other such festivals, mingling with the most grown-up audiences.

On two days each spring, I still tell stories to fourth-graders, not in their classrooms but in a dentist's office in rural Brierfield. It's an unusual setting for storytelling but Dr. Mike Mahan is an unusual man. Not only is he a fine dentist (he often lectures at the School of Dentistry at the University of Alabama in Birmingham, and fellow dentists recognize and admire his meticulous craftsmanship), his other interests are wide-ranging: historic preservation, pipe organ restoration and building, cello playing, participation in reenactments of War Between the States battles, collecting Indian artifacts–and storytelling.

So each spring he arranges to have fourth-graders from Shelby County schools brought to the log cabin waiting room at his creekside office to hear me tell stories. The children, between thirty and forty in each group, sit along the raised edge of the native stone hearth or sit cross-legged on the floor. The chairs and sofa in the waiting room are reserved for teachers, bus drivers and parents.

There's never any mention of dentistry, no personal promotion of any kind. Dr. Mahan does not even remind his guests to brush their teeth. The days, with four sessions each day, are totally devoted to storytelling. I need that yearly contact with my fourth-grade friends: they keep me focused on the pure pleasure of storytelling.

It was Mike Mahan, abetted by our mutual friend Millie Vick, who made and gave me the gold ghost (Jeffrey) pendant I often wear. I'm not sure whose old fillings and bridges went into the making. I was emceeing a Bluegrass festival one night when Mike came on stage, put his arm around my shoulders, and said to the audience, "I bet you did not know that Kathryn is one of my patients."

"Yes," I interrupted, "and I've spent so much money with Mike Mahan that when I die I want my mouth propped open so people can see where my money went."

And then he handed me that gold jewelry. I was almost too chagrined to thank him and Millie properly.

There have been other occasions in my storytelling career when I have been embarrassed, though not the same kind of embarrassment.

One night at the National Storytelling Festival in Jonesborough, I was telling ghost stories up on a hill by the graveyard. The only light came from the flames of a big campfire, and the listeners were spread out in a wide circle around the fire, spread out so far that even their outlines were lost in the darkness. I was in my element, at my storytelling best, recounting the tale of Nellie, a beautiful young girl in Columbus, Mississippi, who fell in love with a tall red-haired stranger.

"Nellie was in downtown Columbus one day watching a bucket

brigade of volunteer firemen fight a fire," I said, "when she fell instantly in love with a handsome young man who was passing water . . ."

I could not believe I had used a rural euphemism for urinating–but I had. How grateful I was for the darkness! I hurried along with my story, hoping my listeners were too citified to know what I had said, but there were a few snickers in the crowd.

It was a long time before I dared tell Nellie's story again.

Then another time I was telling a ghost tale before a large audience when I completely forgot the name of the main character. While I tried to recall his name, I described his appearance in detail, gave a brief history of the town where he lived, spoke highly of his family, even discussed a couple of superstitions that had little or nothing to do with the story. I thought if I kept talking long enough surely the name would come to me. It did not.

I happened to glance at a little boy on the front row; he was holding a copy of the book that contained the story I was trying to tell. It was almost like an answer to prayer, and maybe it was. I stepped to the edge of the stage, asked to borrow his book, looked up the elusive name and went on with my story. The audience, I think, liked the story–and me–even better than they would have if I had told it perfectly. Perfection, fortunately for me, is not a requirement of storytelling.

Some of my most pleasant storytelling experiences have been with groups of Elderhostelers, retirees who spend a week taking college-sponsored courses that interest them. Elderhostelers generally are marked by their youthful spirits, their curiosity, their sense of adventure and their desire to continue learning.

When I am invited to lecture (I dislike that stiff word though I had rather be a lecturer than a presenter, a word both plastic and pompous) at Elderhostel classes, I accept with delight. Because the pupils are of my generation, they can relate to the experiences I talk about, and they understand my references to life in "olden days."

The Elderhostel catalogues give my sessions a variety of topics: "Exploring the Southern Scene," "Are Southerners Really Different?," "I Heard Tell," "Storytelling on a Southern Porch," "Folktales and Superstitions," etc. No matter what the assigned topic is, all I do is tell stories about the South. I have talked a whole week about funeral customs.

The longer I am associated with storytelling the more firmly I believe in its magical, almost mystical powers. A week of storytelling in Wisconsin a good many years ago first made me aware of the strong emotions, the often unexpected reactions, a story can induce.

I had been scheduled to tell stories in a number of different locations during my Wisconsin visit: a rural elementary school, a nursing home, a halfway house for recovering drug abusers, a hospital ward for terminally ill cancer patients and a state prison for youthful offenders. Most of the residents of the nursing home, many of them in wheelchairs, were waiting in an assembly room when I arrived. I was about to begin my stories when an attendant, rather noisily, wheeled an elderly woman into the rear of the room. The woman was slumped against the restraints that held her in the chair, her eyes were closed, and her head wobbled from side to side.

"I don't know why they bothered to bring her," I heard a woman on the front row comment to her companion. "She doesn't even know where she is. Hasn't said a word to anybody in over six months."

During one of my stories, I sang a snatch of a folk song my Aunt Bet used to sing. I know that I cannot sing and I almost never try, but on that occasion the song seemed to fit the tale I was telling. About midway through the chorus, the woman in the rear of the room sat up straight in her wheelchair, caught my eye, smiled and began to sing along with me. It was a strange duet.

As soon as my story ended, I hurried back to speak to her. She held out her hand, and I took it. "My father used to sing that song to me when I was a little girl," she said. "He sang it in Finnish. And I know another verse," and she sang it for me.

I don't know what happened to the woman after I left (I wish I had asked her name), but for a little while she had unloosed the mental restraints that bound her and was alert, alive and happy.

At another stop, a large hospital, about a dozen cancer patients were sitting in a sunny day room. They ranged in age from early twenties to late seventies. Except for the background noise of a television set, which no one was watching, the room was silent. There was no conversation. It was almost as if each patient refused to acknowledge the presence of other human beings.

Yet when I walked in, I sensed a feeling of resentment that a stranger, someone healthy, had presumed to intrude on their privacy under the pretext of coming to entertain them. No one smiled or greeted me.

Looking around that room into the expressionless faces of people who knew that their life span was measured in days or weeks, that death was as close as the I.V. stands beside their chairs, I wondered what kinds of stories I should tell. I began by telling some of Daddy's stories, and I talked about growing up in a small Southern town a long time ago, about my peculiar kinfolks and our eccentric neighbors. I even told them a few ghost stories and then strayed off into superstitions.

At first they tried to ignore me. Then they began to listen and to relax. Finally they laughed.

Soon after I got back home to Selma, I had a letter from the Catholic sister in charge of that ward. After that hour of stories, she wrote me, the patients began to talk to each other for the first time, to talk openly and honestly about their lives, their failures and their successes, their dreams and their fears. They talked about death, their own approaching deaths. They told stories from their childhoods, even sang a few silly songs. They cried together and they laughed together. They became aware of each other and of their need for each other.

"You could feel the love and strength and courage that came into that room and touched their lives," the sister wrote, "all as a result of simple stories."

Of all of my Wisconsin appearances, the visit to the prison concerned me most. My audience would not be truants or hubcap thieves or petty larcenists. The prison, a maximum security facility, housed felons, young men in their teens guilty of armed robbery, grand larceny, drug smuggling, rape and murder.

The warden, I think, was surprised to see my gray hair and to hear my Southern accent. I'm not sure exactly what he expected a storyteller to look and sound like!

"You'll probably have a small audience, not more than a dozen or so," he told me. "This is a voluntary activity, and I don't think many of our inmates will choose to listen to stories! I'll let you stand in the middle of the gym, and your audience can sit on the floor around you. There'll be an armed guard in the corner."

Nothing the warden said allayed my apprehension.

As it turned out, one hundred and seventy-five young men chose to come to the gym to hear stories. Actually, I don't think they came to hear stories–they just came. I looked at them, sprawled out in circles around me, and I wondered what kinds of stories I should tell. Would any of them listen to a gray-haired woman who even talked funny? I glanced around to make sure the guard was on duty, and then I began to tell some of Daddy's stories.

At first the prisoners were amused by my accent. Then they

appeared to ignore me. Gradually they began to listen. They sat up, moved in closer, watched me as I talked. For more than an hour I told stories in that gym. And when I had finished, so many of those prisoners came up to me and said, "Nobody ever told me a story before." I wanted to weep. What difference might it have made in those young lives if someone had taken time to tell them stories, had said, "Come here. I want to tell you a story because I love you"?

That's what storytelling really is all about. Storytelling says, "I love you."

Now, in my seventy-seventh year, I continue to tell stories. Invitations to speak at conventions, to meet with college classes in storytelling, to conduct workshops (I don't believe people can be taught to tell stories; they can only be encouraged to do so), to entertain church groups, and to tell at festivals, still arrive. I'm more selective now about the invitations I accept, more selfish with my time.

If my memory is clear and my arithmetic is accurate, I have told stories in twenty-nine states and two foreign countries (Canada and Germany, both twice) since Jimmy Neil Smith first summoned me to Jonesborough and dubbed me a storyteller.

I'm still surprised, happily surprised, when committee chairmen call long distance (long distance telephone calls were usually harbingers of sad news, critical illnesses or deaths, when I was a child) to invite me to come to some distant city to tell stories. "We'll send your plane tickets and we'll take care of your meals and lodging, of course. What is your fee?"

That question always makes me uncomfortable. I still feel guilty about letting people pay me for doing something that isn't work at all but is pure pleasure. So I usually ask, "How much money do you have?" My fee schedule is very flexible.

Once that unpleasantness is dealt with, I fly off to places I've never been before to tell strangers about my Uncle Wilmer who read lips and had scores of notebooks filled with the conversations he recorded. I tell them about my Aunt Bet who rocked in the shade of a line of ancient oak trees an entire day, singing from a hymn book in her hands with a shotgun across her lap, to keep a highway crew from cutting those trees down; and about our neighbor, Susie Johnson, who had turkeys that could tap dance; about the torture of my piano lessons; and dozens of other tales of growing up in a small Southern town. After a bit, my listeners aren't strangers anymore.

All Things Considered

It must have been in Kentuck, the annual art show and folk festival at Northport, Alabama, that Bo Pittman (I believe his name is Robert, but I'm not sure) heard me tell stories. Bo was manager of WUAL, the Public Radio station in Tuscaloosa, right across the Black Warrior River from Northport. Bo likes storytelling.

Early in 1984, he drove over from Tuscaloosa, bringing the WUAL Producer Sam Hendren with him, to talk to me about doing some commentaries for their station. To be truthful, I think they came to Selma to eat barbecue at Hancock's, to see if the barbecue there was as good as they had heard it was. So while we ate barbecue at Hancock's (Bo, being from North Carolina, praised the taste but was unwise enough to find fault with the texture, said the meat should be chopped fine instead of being served in chunks) we talked about my taping some short pieces for use on their station. I was not very interested.

Except for doing a few spots as political endorsements for friends (only one of the candidates I endorsed ever won), I had not spoken into a microphone since college days. In our senior year at Huntingdon College, my friend and classmate Lucy Bynum and I broadcast a few news reports about happenings at Huntingdon on radio station WSFA in Montgomery. The studios were in the Jefferson Davis Hotel. Our radio venture was short-lived: the dean of women, Mary Ivy Swank, decided it was not proper for two Huntingdon girls, unchaperoned, to be seen coming out of or going into a downtown hotel. It was this same Dean Swank who reminded us at every chapel service, "All a girl has are her health, her education and a reputation." She zealously guarded all three. So our Huntingdon newscasts were canceled.

There was another period, a short one, when I broadcast movie reviews for a theater owner in Montgomery. I was older then, was working as a reporter for The Alabama Journal, so I could enter and depart from the studios without tarnishing Huntingdon's reputation—or my own. I thought about Dean Swank though every time I went to that hotel.

Not only did I lack radio experience, I was reluctant to take on another project. My storytelling was keeping me busy, and requests for presenting my one-woman show, "My Name Is Julia," were increasing. "I don't have time to come to Tuscaloosa to tape or to broadcast," I told Bo. "No problem," he replied. "We'll come to Selma." And they did.

Sam Hendren came over one day with a load of recording equipment, and we set up a temporary studio around my long writing desk. We draped chairs with quilts to muffle the sound, took the telephone off the hook, closed the windows and pulled the curtains. For that initial session, I read parts of a tale I had written for EnviroSouth about a man down in Clarke County, where I grew up, who was the finest tobacco spitter in the whole country. His most amazing feat was when he spit in the eyes of a coiled-up, ready-to-strike rattlesnake, thus saving himself from serious injury or perhaps even death.

It was a good story, one my father used to tell, and Sam did a perfect job of taping it. The Tuscaloosa station used it on the air during a local break in NPR's "Morning Edition," and the tale got some encouraging response. However, the telling sounded stiff and cold, as if I were reading the piece, which I was. That was the last time I ever read a prepared script for one of my commentaries. I didn't even use notes. Sam and I would decide what I would talk about and I would tell the tale to him, tell it naturally and relaxed, as if he and I were the only people who would ever hear it. I felt comfortable doing the taping that way.

Later I had a listener tell me, "When I first started listening to you, there'd be pauses in the broadcast, and I'd think my radio had gone bad. I didn't want to miss anything you were saying, so I'd start to shake or hit the radio, but, before I did you'd be speaking again. Took me a while to get used to your deliberate, unhurried delivery." He probably guessed that during those pauses I was trying to think what to say next.

Only recently a listener suggested that my storytelling reflected my father's style: the slow cadence of his rocking chair and the pauses while he puffed on his pipe.

Sam and I did not do all of the taping in our makeshift home studio. Sometimes we would go to Cahaba and I'd talk about that deserted town, or we'd stroll through old graveyards and I'd read epitaphs. He would come over about once a month, and we'd do four or five commentaries, enough to give WUAL one to air each week until we had another session. Somehow we nearly always managed to eat lunch at Hancock's. One of our segments was taped in that popular, noisy place.

Sam, being a perfectionist, knew the quality of the tapes would improve if we did them in the studio in Tuscaloosa, a trip of eighty miles from Selma, so we began to schedule sessions there. I often had business in Tuscaloosa (conferences with the editors at The University of Alabama Press, research in the University of Alabama library, autographing my books in bookstores, storytelling in the schools, workshops for adults, etc.), and my son was on the staff of The Tuscaloosa News, so it was really no hardship for me to include an hour or so of taping in my schedule.

I had been doing commentaries on WUAL more than a year when

Bo Pittman sent a tape of one of my tales to "All Things Considered," the afternoon program broadcast by National Public Radio from Washington. One November afternoon in 1985, sitting right in my kitchen, I heard myself telling about a terrible hailstorm in my home town of Thomasville, hail so big and strong it knocked the eyes out of the goldfish in the pool in Vance and Myrtie Norred's front yard. I don't know whether it was the story or my Southern delivery they liked, but NPR asked Bo to send more tapes of my tales.

For eighteen months NPR aired my commentaries, some thirty-three of them scattered through that period. The letters began arriving, more letters than I ever received about all my books put together. The first came from New York City. "Ma'am," it said, "you sure restored my faith in language and story to convey magic. Very graceful, the way you put hail and goldfishes' eyes into relationship."

During those months on NPR, I talked about standard Southern topics such as grits and kudzu, linking each to my small-town childhood, and I also talked about making frog houses in damp sand, piano lessons, family photographs, a fancy green rubber bathing suit that split, early morning sounds, iced tea, chicken pie, even country graveyards and fleas.

Letters came from thirty-four states, including Alaska and Hawaii, with my pieces on grits, honeysuckle and frog houses prompting the most numerous responses. Reading the letters, I became aware that the listeners were less concerned with the contents of the commentaries than with the delivery: it wasn't what I said, it was how I said it. From Massachusetts came a letter saying, "Your gentle accent and delivery are truly the voice of the region of my childhood recollections of refinement and good humor, so unlike the 'fiddle-dee-dee, Miz Scarlett' caricature heard too often in poorly acted dramas. Thank you for giving the nation a glimpse of the South's finer side."

Two families wrote of rediscovering the delight of making frog houses after hearing me talk on the subject. I had a letter from another listener protesting my cruelty in pinching off the tails of lightning bugs and sticking those glowing tails in the tops of my frog houses to provide illumination. He suggested that I might also like to try pulling wings off flies!

A Presbyterian minister wrote of listening to me while driving at sunset along a North Carolina expressway. "That sunset, your lovely Alabama voice and the memories you stirred made me forget recent pastoral weariness and renewed my soul. Thank you for being on the air to bless that day's end."

A musicology teacher at an Illinois university, born in Georgia but gone from his native state for thirty-five years, wanted his young daughters to "hear in those caressing R's and gentle modulations the sounds I had thought were forgotten from my childhood," and a Texan wrote that when I speak he hears his south Alabama grandmother telling stories. Descriptions and comments about my voice varied, but the one I cherish said, "Your voice is so rich. I feel as though I am savoring a deliciously thick custard as I listen to you. It melts on the tongue, envelopes it and slowly evaporates down the throat. I want it to last forever."

"It is so refreshing to hear a bit of charming nostalgia amid the raucous jangle of current society," wrote a listener from New Mexico, and another listener commented, "Your observations remind me of the really important things in life, far removed from the hectic pace I sometimes fall into."

In one of my commentaries I talked about Lige Danzy, a black man who used to come sit in the shade of the chinaberry tree in our back yard and weave baskets of white oak splits. As a little girl, I liked to watch him work, and I liked even more the tales he told and the songs he sang. Several days after NPR ran that piece, I had a letter from Lige's kin, now living in Michigan. The writer's husband had been born in Thomasville long after Lige died. Though he never knew Lige, when he heard the words Thomasville and Danzy (his mother's maiden name) on the radio, he called his mother and she assured him that the basketmaker he had heard me talk about was their "Cousin 'Lijah." "It was a unique and enjoyable experience for my husband and his Mom and Dad to hear your story. They shared your nostalgia," the woman wrote. I hope they got together and told stories about Lige. I still have one of the big baskets he made more than seventy years ago.

The most unusual letter of all came from someone I've known and loved since her childhood, Betty Ehlert McManus, who grew up in Selma and now lives in San Diego. Betty and her husband, Tom, had bought a house in a different part of the city and had completed the major part of their move when Tom was called out of town on business. Betty decided to finish the move herself, loading the final items into her small, two-door Japanese car.

In the late afternoon, physically and mentally exhausted, she drove toward her new home, took the wrong exit off the freeway and became hopelessly lost in a maze of unfamiliar streets. The harder she tried to find her way out, the more wrong turns she made. She began to cry, tears of weariness and frustration and loneliness. When the tears blurred her vision so that she could not drive safely, she pulled over to the curb, turned on the radio and began to sob.

"Then you came to my rescue," she wrote me. "There you were on All Things Considered telling me a story about Selma and Mabry Street where I grew up, about Live Oak Cemetery where dear ones are buried and about the Hotel Albert where I used to stand outside the barber shop and watch old men get their haircuts. You were my compass. I wasn't lost anymore. Thank you for being there."

Is there an explanation for my basketmaker friend's family happening to hear me talk about him on NPR? Or for Betty McManus tuning in to a familiar voice to guide her home? I wish I knew!

Of course, not everyone liked my commentaries. Some of my mail spoke of my stories as "terribly outdated, an example of facile dismissal, with stereotyped labels of human beings who need help" and of me as "indulging in thoughtless nostalgia." My children delighted in that last phrase. They often ask me, "What are you doing today? Indulging in thoughtless nostalgia?" I often plead guilty to the charge.

One man, in the late spring of 1987, wrote to NPR, "Regarding the stories of Mrs. Kathyrn Tucker Windham, when I hear her elegant Southern accent, justified or not, all I see is a beaten down race of people mowing her friends' lawns." Although he seemed unconcerned about who mowed my lawn, I wrote to inform him that I still performed that chore myself as do many of my friends.

Perhaps the letter (it came from Mouth of Wilson, Virginia, an intriguing place name) had nothing to do with it, but soon afterwards NPR stopped using my commentaries. The producers may have decided my pieces were not politically correct, or, as they told one listener who called to inquire, it was time other sections of the country were represented. I had never had any correspondence, certainly nothing so formal as a contract, when NPR started using my recollections, and there was no correspondence when they stopped, so I don't know who made what decisions or why.

Tuscaloosa's WUAL continued to use my comments sporadically, whenever Sam Hendren and I could arrange a taping session, and WLRH, Huntsville's NPR station, still uses one of my tales every Saturday on Judy and Harry Watters's Sundial program. Sam sends them tapes from the master reels he has in Tuscaloosa. Sam is a very remarkable fellow: he can quote verbatim nearly every tale I ever told. Sometimes he begins quoting, mimicking my tone of voice and speech pattern, just to tease me, knowing full well that much of the material he is reciting has long ago catapulted into the uncharted chasms of my mind.

Just as Sam is responsible for taping my stories in the first place, and for preserving the master tapes, he is also responsible for having produced audio tapes, four of them, of my "best" stories. I had received requests for information about the availability of such tapes as well as letters urging me to "preserve your stories and your authentic Southern voice" for future generations, and Sam thought it would be a good idea. The first edition of what we called "Recollections" was produced to give as premiums for donors to WUAL's annual fund drive, and its success prompted Sam to edit and produce three more volumes of my comments. The station continues to use them as fund-raisers as does the Huntsville station, and I have a supply stashed in my garage to use in filling other requests.

People listening to those tapes comment as favorably about Sam's sound effects as about the stories themselves. Sam, careful craftsman that he is, spent countless hours seeking out exactly the authentic sounds needed to enhance the stories: birds singing, crickets chirping, a swamp filled with frogs in full voice, a steam locomotive, a Model T Ford, children splashing in water, thunder, etc. He calls it "getting the proper ambiance"; others speak of "the wonderful sound effects that bridge the stories."

In 1991, WUAL was given the Gabriel Award by the National Catholic Association of Broadcasters and Communications for "Christmas in Alabama," an hour-long program which Sam produced and I narrated. Other winners that year included Ken Burns's Civil War series and ABC's 20/20 news programs. Sam and I were right proud of being up there with the big boys.

My taped "Recollections" continue to bring me new friends and new experiences. One night in the spring of 1993 an artist from upper New York state called. His name was Evan Wilson, he told me, and he grew up in Tuscaloosa but had lived in the north for a good many years. "I listened to a tape of you talking about honeysuckle. It made me so homesick I wept. I'll be going down to Mobile soon to see my mother. May I come to Selma to meet you?" he asked. Of course I invited him to come.

Evan is very tall, slender and bearded and is a part of my children's generation. He had never been to Selma before, and he was charmed by the beauty and the diversity of the town. He was interested in everything, asked questions, listened and took many photographs. He was a delightful guest.

Upon his return to New York state, he called to ask if he might come back to Selma to paint my portrait. "I'll need for you to sit for me for two days," he told me, "if you can spare me that much time." Nobody had ever offered to paint my portrait before (I'm not sure I even know any portrait painters), and the possibility of having one done had never occurred to me. "If you don't want to do it, I'll understand," Evan told me. Of course I wanted to do it!

So Evan brought his wife and two little boys, the same ages as my grandsons, to Selma with him to paint my portrait. His family stayed at a nearby motel where there was a swimming pool, coming to my house every now and then to play with my grandsons' toys, to check on the progress of the painting, and to do artwork of their own on the backs of proof pages saved for that very purpose. Their pictures are still displayed on my refrigerator.

Posing was not as difficult as I had imagined it would be. I sat in an old wicker rocker, one that rocked me many a mile in our home in Thomasville, and I wore a comfortable blue and white striped dress, the straw hat with feathers that has become my storytelling trademark, and

Mike Mahan's gold Jeffrey around my neck. Evan did pencil sketches once he was satisfied with the lighting, and we chatted and laughed a lot as he worked. He took several color photographs, too, though he dislikes doing portraits from photographs.

A few weeks later, when he and his family returned from a vacation on Alabama's Gulf Coast, he brought me two of the pencil sketches, elegantly framed, and my portrait, so like me that I was startled. As I look at them, admire them, I wonder why this stranger, this talented young artist, would give me such treasures, wonder how a simple story about the fragrance of honeysuckle could have prompted his gifts of love.

Perhaps it is all a part of the magic of storytelling. Perhaps.

Miss Julia

Nearly sixty years elapsed between my acting debut at age seven and my second appearance on stage. Miss Carrie Head, my first-grade teacher, gave me my initial acting role when she cast me as Mammy in her dramatization of "Epaminondas and His Auntie," one of my favorite stories. The play was to be a part of our class program at a Parent–Teacher Association meeting.

The title role of Epaminondas was assigned to Thomas Lloyd Griffin (everybody called him Bitty) who was my seatmate and was the first boy I ever loved. I was happy about the prospect of appearing on stage with him (playing the role of his mother disturbed my childish sensibilities not at all), and I'm pretty sure he shared my feelings. Since we were both familiar with Epaminondas's stupid and funny misadventures as he brought home the gifts his Auntie gave him, we learned our lines quickly.

We did the show in blackface. Back then, in the mid-1920s, nobody raised ethical questions about sensitivity or political correctness or racism when two white children blacked their faces to play the roles of colored characters. Our mothers had the more practical concerns of getting the makeup off our clothes and out of our hair.

Things went well until the day of the performance. After our final rehearsal, Miss Head said to me, "Kathryn, I've decided to change the ending. Instead of having the curtain fall as Epaminondas steps in his

Mammy's pies, I want you to come on stage and shake your finger at him as though you are very angry. Then I want you to sit in this chair, turn him across your lap, and spank him."

I was shocked. But I was an obedient child, brought up knowing better than to question the edicts of parents or of teachers, so I, though reluctant, agreed to do as Miss Head requested. We did not have time to practice the new ending.

Every seat in the auditorium was filled for the meeting, and our first grade won the attendance banner for having the most parents and friends present. Each part of the program received adequate applause, but when our play ended with my turning Bitty across my knees and spanking him, the laughter and the applause rattled the windows. Oh, how grateful I was when the curtain rolled down!

The sense of indignity and of humiliation must have been worse for Bitty than it was for me. We did not talk about it. Our relationship was never the same again.

After that unfortunate experience, any acting aspirations I may have had withered away. I did play a few minor roles in high school productions. Our school had a small enrollment and all students, no matter how lacking in interest or in talent, were expected to participate. In college I tried out for a play or two, but I was never good enough to be included in the casts.

Then, almost sixty years after my portrayal of Mammy, the spirit of a forceful and determined woman, Julia Strudwick Tutwiler, entered my life and thrust me on stage again.

I had grown up hearing about Julia Tutwiler. In our fourth-grade history class, we learned that she visited jails and prisons, devoted her life to teaching, and used her influence to open the doors of the University of Alabama to women students. We also learned all seven verses of the state song, "Alabama," which she wrote, and we sang her song (but not all seven verses!) at every school assembly program. I wonder if any schoolchildren now know and sing "Alabama."

My friend and classmate, Patsy Dumas, and I made a poster to illustrate Miss Tutwiler's song, and we won a blue ribbon and a cash award for our efforts. That cash award gave me a kindly feeling for Miss Tutwiler.

A great many years passed before I had any more serious thoughts about this Alabama woman whom I never knew, who died two years before I was born.

Then in the spring of 1974, I was invited to speak at the annual meeting of the Alabama Federation of Women's Clubs, a meeting to be held at the University of Alabama in Tuscaloosa. The general theme of the convention was "Women Of Action." In casting about for a subject for my talk, Miss Tutwiler came rather forcefully to my mind. She, truly a woman of action, would be the ideal subject, especially for a talk on the very campus where she campaigned so vigorously and finally successfully for the admission of women students, and in the very building that bore her name.

But though I had the perfect subject, I could find very little information about Miss Tutwiler's life. There were a few paragraphs about her in several history texts, there was a scholarly book dealing with her contributions to social reform in Alabama, and there were batches of yellowed, often repetitious newspaper feature stories highlighting her accomplishments, but that was about all. The material was mighty meager.

I did manage to gather up enough facts and comments to fill my allotted time on the program, but all during my search, I kept thinking, "Somebody should write a book about this amazing woman." I never once imagined that the assignment would go to me, that Miss Julia would virtually order me to take on that responsibility.

But at some point during my research, Miss Julia began to haunt me. Even after my talk to the club women was over and I had discarded my notes, I continued to be aware of her powerful presence. I would hear "Alabama" played or sung on improbable occasions. Strangers would be introduced to me as, "She's a kinswoman of Miss Julia." Her name would leap out at me from printed pages. Women would come up to me in restaurants or stores or on the sidewalks in other towns to comment on my talk about Miss Tutwiler. I would overhear her name in a crowded theater. It was almost as if she were saying, "I will not let you forget me. I will not! You will write my story." She was an exceedingly strong-willed woman.

And so I began gathering information about Miss Tutwiler. The more I learned about her, the more I admired her intellect, her energy, her total devotion to the causes she espoused. For ten years, prodded by her stubborn spirit, I collected Tutwiler material. I sought out her former students, many of them in nursing homes, and heard their recollections of their beloved teacher; I read thick files in the Department of Archives and History; I corresponded with her kinfolks in other states; I listened to hours of interviews, tape-recorded decades ago, with her former coworkers, friends and pupils at Alabama Normal College; I pored over scrapbooks and old college catalogues at Livingston University; I established temporary residence in the Alabama reference room at the Gorgas Library at the University of Alabama; I visited with Livingston residents and with family members who had Tutwiler tales to tell; I struggled to decipher distressingly small collections of her letters (her handwriting was atrocious); and I gathered anecdotes wherever I could find them.

My Tutwiler material filled notebooks and overflowed into boxes. Finally I was ready to begin writing the book. Or so I thought. I had blocked out some weeks of uncluttered time for writing, had organized my research and had even made an outline.

There was only one problem: Miss Julia refused to be put into a book. That determined woman who had hovered around the fringes of my mind for nearly ten years, who at times seemed to possess me, defied all my efforts to write a book about her. It was as if she spoke plainly to me: "I will not be confined to the pages of a book! I want to be free, moving about. I want to be alive, if even for a little while, as you speak my words."

When I protested that I had never written a play, that I knew nothing about writing dialogue, and that I was no actress, I could almost hear her quoting Scripture, as she so often did, could hear her repeating God's words to the reluctant prophet Jeremiah, "Behold, I have put my words in thy mouth."

And so Miss Julia Tutwiler moved from the fringes of my mind into the very center of my consciousness. So completely did she claim me at times that my children and my friends often asked, "Is Kathryn at home today or is Miss Julia there?"

She was a rigid taskmaster. I wrote and rewrote and rewrote the script for the one-woman performance. After the sixth revision, I took the typed pages to Montgomery to ask my friend Allen Rankin to read them. Allen was one of the finest writers I've ever known, and I respected his opinion completely.

We sat on a sunny porch, Allen and I, and he read the script slowly, dropping each finished page beside his chair. He made no comments as he read. Impatient to know his reaction, I tried to study his face for a clue, but he did not change his expression. As the last page fluttered to the floor, Allen turned to me and exclaimed, "My God, Kathryn! That's about the sorriest piece of writing I've ever read! You can surely do better than that!"

He gave me some suggestions for improvement, and I gathered up

Me in my costume as I waited to perform at Tutwiler Prison.

JEAN MARTIN

my manuscript and came home. I do not doubt that Miss Julia shared Allen's opinion though she certainly would not have used his words. I lost count of the number of revisions I made in the script, but the more I wrote, the closer I felt to my subject.

Word of my project spread around, as such things always do in small towns, and I was invited to give excerpts from my show (by then it had a title, "My Name Is Julia") to the Agape Club at the Presbyterian Church, the Rotary Club and one or two other such local organizations. I welcomed the opportunities to practice on homefolks. My major concern at that point was getting a costume together.

My Depression-oriented compulsion to "save things" stood me in good stead. In the back of a closet crammed with my children's costumes from their school days performances (I still have a fuzzy yellow chicken outfit my oldest child wore in her earliest dance recital and a beaded Indian dress my other daughter wore in a first-grade play) I found a jacket of dark, heavy material, a black straw bonnet I had bought for a quarter at a yard sale years ago, a commodious if battered purse, and a pair of lace-up shoes with pointed toes. All I needed were a long skirt and a wig (my gray hair was the proper color for the role—there just was not enough of it!). The late Betty Morrow, my dear friend, volunteered to make my skirt from remnants of black serge, precisely the inexpensive and serviceable kind of material Miss Julia would have selected, found in the recesses of that same blessed closet. The skirt was by far the most authentic part of Miss Julia's attire. However, with the wig topped by the bonnet, tied under my chin by wide grosgrain ribbons, and with the addition of a walking cane, I did not look too unlike the photographs of Miss Julia.

My local audiences were attentive and complimentary, as I knew they would be no matter what the caliber of my performance. I was sure Selma groups would be supportive, but I was very uneasy about how

"My Name Is Julia" would be received out-of-town.

The first big test came on an early November Sunday afternoon in 1983 when I was invited to present an abbreviated version of the play at the dedication of the addition to the Julia S. Tutwiler Library at Livingston University, the school where she spent thirty years of her life. The citizens of Livingston were quite familiar with the life of Miss Julia, had grown up hearing stories about her, and I knew they would not hesitate to call attention to any errors or shortcomings in my portrayal of the woman whom many of them considered to be a borderline saint.

All during October I agonized over the approaching engagement. I railed out against Miss Julia, reminding her that she was solely responsible for my miserable predicament, that I had never intended to be thrust into the unwanted role of actress. As the November date approached, I had diarrhea. I broke out in a rash. I continued to hurl bitter barbs at Miss Julia, placing the blame for the approaching disaster squarely on her. I cried often and loudly. I suppose it was wailing more than simple crying. I would have sought solace in strong drink, but I knew Miss Julia, staunch supporter of the Women's Christian Temperance Union that she was, would never tolerate such behavior.

I drove over to Livingston the day before the scheduled performance and checked into a small motel. I almost registered as Miss Julia S. Tutwiler. I made so many changes in the script that I wore holes in the pages. I tape-recorded passage after passage, playing each one back to a critical listener–me. I tried on my costume a dozen times. I practiced walking with a cane. I stood in front of a tall mirror and watched as Miss Julia spoke her lines, over and over and over. It was a miserable twenty-four hours. And the worst was yet to come.

Sunday afternoon, clad in my full costume, I drove over to the University campus long before the appointed hour for the presentation.

I found a parking place near the library but not right in front, and I sat in the car, alternately reviewing my lines and bewailing the curious chain of circumstances that had propelled me into the present predicament. When the mercifully small crowd began to gather, I took up my purse and cane and entered the library.

Dr. Neil Snider, the librarian, and other local dignitaries greeted me and escorted me to a folding chair on the front row. I tried to appear calm and composed, tried not to let my hosts become aware of how grateful my trembling knees were to have a cane to lean on.

After my introduction, I walked up to the lectern and turned to face my audience. It was then that I saw, staring straight at me, a life-size portrait of Miss Julia S. Tutwiler! Her piercing eyes never left my face, and her firm lips, though unmoving, seemed to say to me, "I expect you to do well, to do very well."

Not for one instant during the entire hour was I unaware of her presence. I wondered as I took on her personality, as I pretended to be Miss Julia, how she would react to my interpretation of her life story. All through the performance I tried to avoid looking at the portrait. Only after I had spoken the final lines did I gaze up at her. I could have been mistaken (I was very weary and emotionally drained), but I think I saw Miss Julia smile slightly and nod.

With the assurance that she approved of the drama I had created, my later performances of "My Name Is Julia" were more relaxed, less stressful. My diarrhea disappeared and so did my rash.

In the spring of 1984, I was invited to give a Sunday afternoon performance in Greensboro where Miss Julia had close family ties. I knew several of her nieces, nephews and cousins would likely be in the audience, and I also knew that a few of her kinspeople were old enough to remember Miss Julia quite well. My nervous ailments threatened to return.

During the social hour that followed my presentation, I overheard one of the Tutwiler family members comment, "I think she did a good job of acting, don't you? Her voice sounded a great deal like Cousin Julia, and some of the expressions she used were exactly like Cousin Julia. But don't you remember Cousin Julia as being stouter than Mrs. Windham?"

I was as pleased as if I had won an Academy Award.

My greatest compliment comes when a member of the audience hurries up to me at the conclusion of the play, stops suddenly and says with an embarrassed laugh, "I almost made a fool of myself; I almost asked you if you remember teaching my mother at Livingston." I know then that my portrayal has been honest, that Miss Julia did come alive.

On two occasions Miss Julia has been invited to make brief speeches to the Alabama Legislature, and on each occasion she chided the politicians for their failure to enact education and prison reform measures, the same reforms for which the real Miss Julia lobbied more than a century ago. Though her words caught and held the attention of the present legislators, those politicians ignored her pleas for reform, treating the visit as only a distracting curiosity.

The initial appearance before the Legislature (May 1, 1984) was followed several nights later by a benefit performance at Huntingdon College. Proceeds went to Julia Tutwiler Prison for Women at Wetumpka to support the prison ministry there.

The chapel at Huntingdon was comfortably filled for the occasion. The director of the State Department of Corrections and his family were on the front row, and Allen Rankin came to see how well I had followed his suggestions for rewriting the script. There were printed programs, and someone had created an authentic stage set of the 1913 period.

The highlight of the evening was the music by a band from Speigner Prison. Under the direction of their leader, the prisoners played a medley of old-fashioned tunes before the play began, and they entertained again with century-old music during intermission. Inspired by their music, I gave one of my best performances.

After I left the stage at the end of the play, my host for the evening called me to come back. "The members of the band want to play a special song for Miss Julia," he announced.

So the audience remained seated and I returned to the stage expecting to hear a chorus or two of "Alabama." What I heard instead was a blaring, rocking rendition of "Baby, Baby, I Love You" with vocals by the group's lead singer, a dark man with a deep bass voice.

I'm not sure how Miss Julia would have reacted, but I wanted to burst out laughing at the incongruity of the serenade. Only by the greatest effort was I able to hold on to my composure, and I dared not look at any of my friends in the audience; they were even more amused than I was.

Several band members and the vocalist left their places in the orchestra pit and gathered around me on stage as they played and sang the song over and over and over again. It finally dawned on me that they were continuing their alleged tribute to me solely to delay their return to prison, so I interrupted their performance, thanked them profusely and hurried off stage.

During the next three years, Miss Julia and I made dozens of appearances around the state, presenting our play (most often the short version but a good many full performances, too) at colleges, universities, historical societies, AAUW events, Methodist gatherings and such. I made a few changes in the script, nothing major, off and on, and Miss Julia and I grew to have a good understanding, a pleasant relationship. We were comfortable with each other.

Our names went up on a theater marquee for the first time in May 1985, when a performance of "My Name Is Julia" was included in the festivities marking the opening of Selma's Performing Arts Center.

The center, housed in the old Walton Theater complex, was a gift to the city from Larry Striplin, a local industrialist who grew up in Selma. In its refurbished glory, the building bore small resemblance to the theater where my three children spent uncounted Saturday mornings with their beloved nurse, Viola, watching cowboy movies. This was back in the 1950s, back in the days of racial segregation, so, since Viola was not allowed to sit downstairs, the children sat in the colored balcony with her, joining other nurses and their charges there.

Miss Julia would surely have been pleased with the changed role of the building, but she would likely have been embarrassed to see her name publicly displayed above the entrance. I was not embarrassed. I took several pictures of the marquee, but I can't find them now.

In early 1987 came an invitation from the Museum of Contemporary Art in Los Angeles to bring my play there in May. I don't know how they ever heard of me or of Miss Julia out there on the West Coast, but the invitation was authentic. I was skeptical, just as I had been suspicious of the invitation to tell tales at the National Storytelling Festival some years earlier, so I investigated thoroughly.

A knowledgeable young woman, Julie Lazar, who was curator for performing arts, went patiently over all the details with me and assured me that though the museum patrons were not familiar with Miss Julia or with me, they were eager to become acquainted with both of us. The young curator was so filled with confidence and so reassuring that the uneasy symptoms of a return of my earlier stage fright afflictions vanished completely.

I suffered a sudden relapse when I saw the MOCA building: it, to me, was cold and sterile, threatening and foreboding. As I was escorted around the place and was taken to see exhibits in other buildings, I wondered if people who were attracted to such art would find anything of interest in the simple stories I had to tell or would be impressed by—or even understand—Miss Julia Tutwiler.

I wondered what Miss Julia, who had visited the art museums in Europe and who often lectured on the works of the masters, would say about the collections of art I was seeing: the carcass of an ancient peanut-parching machine sitting alone in a deserted hall; a bare room filled with pale blue light; tall stalks of bamboo against a chain-link fence shrouded periodically by hissing bursts of steam from underground pipes; a deep, jagged ditch exposing the foundation of an old building; and more, much more.

If I worried—and I did—about how a sophisticated, metropolitan, contemporary-culture-oriented audience would react to the story of a long-dead Alabama woman told by an unknown, untrained "actress," my worries vanished as soon as I spoke the opening lines: I felt Miss Julia's presence as I had never felt it before. Her spirit must have moved among the audience, too. They listened, they laughed at all the proper places, they sighed in sympathy with Miss Julia, a few even wept, and when the show ended, they gave Miss Julia a heartening ovation.

I came home thinking the California foray might mark the end of my close association with Miss Julia, that she might be satisfied at last and would set me free to follow other interests. That was wishful and foolish thinking: she was not nearly through with me. To be honest, I would have missed her if our relationship had been severed completely.

So I continued to do performances of "My Name Is Julia" around Alabama. The requests for appearances came often enough to keep me in practice and to remind me that Miss Julia still required and expected my services. She no longer dominated my life—but she was present.

It was not until 1990 that I suddenly understood, or thought I understood, why Miss Julia was not ready to depart gracefully: the one hundred and fiftieth anniversary of her birth (August 15, 1841) was approaching, and she wanted a proper celebration.

I don't know what kinds of birthday parties Miss Julia had during her lifetime, but her one hundred and fiftieth anniversary observance was outstanding. It began in early 1991 with newspaper stories calling attention to the approaching anniversary, and continued throughout the year as her admirers all around Alabama sponsored events in her honor.

The rumpled, marked-up, tattered script which I had carried around in Miss Julia's purse for seven years was published, quite elegantly, by the Birmingham Public Library. For the first time, libraries and interested individuals could purchase "My Name Is Julia," and I no longer had to worry about losing the only copy of the play.

The library marked its publication of the play with an autograph reception followed by the presentation of the drama. In the audience that night was the late James Hatcher, founder of Town and Gown Theater, and director/producer for that organization for forty-one years. We were longtime friends, and I had gone to him for advice when Miss Julia first began prodding me to tell her life story on stage. During that visit he made suggestions for staging, and when I expressed my feelings of inadequacy for taking on such a role, pointing out my complete lack of theatrical training, his advice was, "Trust your instincts."

After watching my performance at the Birmingham Library that October night in 1991, Hatch paid me one of the highest compliments I have ever received. "You and Charles Laughton are the only performers I've ever seen who could stand almost still on the stage and hold the complete attention of an audience for an hour," he told me. His praise made me so giddy I did not return to normal for days.

In conjunction with the publication of "My Name Is Julia," and the celebration of her one hundred and fiftieth birthday, Dr. Marvin Whiting, archivist for the library, mounted an exhibition of material chronicling the life and work of Miss Julia, possibly the largest display of Tutwiler memorabilia ever assembled and displayed. There were also tributes to Miss Julia sponsored by the Sumter County Fine Arts Council in cooperation with Livingston University, by the Auburn University Center for the Arts and Humanities, by the Friends of the Alabama Archives and by other groups, but the biggest celebration of all was at Julia Tutwiler Prison for Women at Wetumpka.

When I first began to plan events for Miss Julia's one hundred and fiftieth year, I knew that nothing marking the occasion would be more fitting or would please the honoree more than a birthday party for the inmates at the prison that bears her name.

The warden, Shirlie Lobmiller, was enthusiastic about the idea when I went to confer with her (no matter how many times I visit that prison, I always cringe when the heavy barred door slams shut behind me), and we agreed to celebrate late afternoon on August 15, Miss Julia's natal day. The festivities would take place outside on the softball field so all the inmates could attend, there would be colored streamers for decoration, party hats and favors for everybody, and I, dressed as Miss Julia, would make a brief, very brief, talk.

A few days before the scheduled party, I went back to the prison to make sure no problems had developed. The warden called in the recreation director to go over details with me. She assured me everything was on schedule.

"The cake is going to be perfect," she said. I had visions of a cake baked in the shape of Alabama or perhaps a large sheet cake with a map of the state embossed on it.

"It's going to be baked in tiers and decorated with clowns," she explained.

Clowns? I said nothing–it was their party. "And some of the girls want to put on a little entertainment," she continued.

"That's fine," I replied. "Will they sing Miss Julia's song, 'Alabama'?"

"No," the woman replied. "They're going to do 'Jail House Rock.' The group did it five years ago, and it was a big hit. We have all the original cast back now, so they want to do it again."

"Good," I managed to say. It was their party.

So we had a cake decorated with clowns instead of one depicting the state, and we had one of the world's most enthusiastic productions of "Jail House Rock" (the dancing and the beat were so enticing that even usually detached newspaper reporters joined in) instead of a decorous rendition of Miss Julia's "Alabama." But it was fun. Everybody had cake and ice cream (a rare treat for the six hundred or so inmates), and Miss Julia had an opportunity to mingle with and talk to the prisoners. So young they were, most of them, so very young!

"I lived in Tutwiler Hall when I graduated from the University of Alabama," one of them told me, and another said, "I read your *Serigamy of Stories* when I was in jail in north Alabama," and over and over I heard, "Please pray for me. Please pray for me." Less heartbreaking were the reassuring observations, "You don't look like you're a hundred and fifty years old!" and, "I never would have believed I'd meet anybody one hundred and fifty years old–you sure don't look it; mighty spry for somebody that old!"

I hope Miss Julia approved of her party, didn't consider it too frivolous. At the time, I also hoped she would be satisfied with my efforts to "maker her alive" and would stop interfering with my life, but she wasn't ready to leave me alone, not quite yet. Requests for performances of "My Name Is Julia" continued to come not only ırom Alabama but from as far as Indiana and New York state. She and I traveled to

Indianapolis in March, 1993, for a program at the state prison for women there. The inmates, bored and uninterested when the presentation started, were cheering and applauding Miss Julia's reform efforts before the show ended. Then in February, 1994, I took Miss Julia to the Heckschere Museum in Huntington, New York, for an audience more staid but no less appreciative of Miss Julia's goals and attainments.

Although she may have been pleased with my efforts to portray her on stage, she apparently wanted to make sure that my interpretation of her life would survive after my death. She wanted her story preserved on videotape.

So for several months Brent Davis, a producer, camera crews and other technicians from Alabama Public Television studios at the University of Alabama filmed scenes from "My Name Is Julia," documenting locations associated with her reform movements and recording my comments about her life. I can only assume that Miss Julia prodded them into taking on the project.

We filmed on location at the white frame church at Havana (Hale County) where Miss Julia is buried beside her father, at the school in Livingston where she devoted so many loving years, at the women's prison that bears her name, in Montgomery where she dared attend legislative sessions, and in the television studios on the campus of the University of Alabama.

Putting Miss Julia on tape gave me an opportunity to talk about an episode of her life which I learned of too late to put into the script of "My Name Is Julia" but which I knew should be included in her biography.

On one of my information-gathering trips to Livingston, Dr. Neil Snider, director of Livingston University's Julia Tutwiler Library, introduced me to a retired black schoolteacher, Mrs. Ida Sampson Gayle, who told me a story about her father's education.

Charles Sylvester Sampson, her father, and several other black students were taught in a brush arbor school in Sumter County, a school conducted by a Northern missionary. Young Sampson wanted to become a teacher himself, but he could not teach in Alabama's public schools unless he passed the state teacher's examination.

Miss Julia, impressed by his bright mind and his earnest desire to teach, agreed to tutor him and two of his companions. Although it cannot be documented, Miss Julia's act of kindness in tutoring those students doubtless made Livingston the first integrated campus in Alabama.

With Miss Julia's guidance, the young man did pass the examination to get his teacher's certificate, and at his tutor's urging, he later enrolled in and graduated from the State Normal School in Montgomery in 1896.

Charles Sylvester Sampson's desire for learning has been passed along to his children and grandchildren and their families with the result that his descendants have graduated from thirty-six universities or colleges with degrees in law, medicine, music, education, speech pathology, nursing, counseling, electronic engineering, computer science and other fields.

"None of us now living ever knew Miss Tutwiler," Mrs. Gayle told me, "but we all call her blessed."

That story itself merits a whole documentary, it seems to me.

There were interruptions and delays in our taping schedule, and I wondered how Brent and his coworkers would ever assemble the segments into a smooth-flowing, hour-long show. I still don't know how they did it, but they did. "Let Her Own Works Praise Her" was shown on Alabama Public Television during prime time on December 15, 1993 (a half-page announcement, including a photograph of me in costume, appeared in that week's TV Guide), and the program has been

On her 150th birthday, August 15, 1991, Miss Julia hosted a party, complete with ice cream and cake, at the prison that bears her name.

rerun several times since then. The University of Alabama Center for Public Television made copies of the tape available to public libraries across the state, a move that would surely have pleased Miss Julia.

As I have spoken the lines from the play on stage and have watched my actions and heard my words on the tape, I have been amazed that what started as a simple luncheon talk a bit over two decades ago has spread in so many directions, has involved me in so many new experiences, enriching my life.

I can almost hear Miss Julia saying, "See? I did put my words in your mouth, just the way I promised."

The Falls and Other Tribulations

A distinction to ponder: children and young people fall, but older people "have a fall." I am not sure at what age the terminology officially changes, but change it does. I first became aware of the distinction when I had a fall. Three of them in fact. I was past sixty-five.

I had been invited to make the Laymen's Day address (probably now Layperson's Day, if I must be politically correct–which I hate!) at the United Methodist Church in Alabaster, a small town some twenty miles south of Birmingham. Since I was reared in the United Methodist Church, known back then as the Methodist Episcopal Church, South, I felt comfortable accepting the invitation. I thought how pleased my parents would be to know that I was to occupy the pulpit at a Methodist Church. Unfortunately I failed to recall that my mother, a very wise and devout woman, used to say, "Only ordained ministers of the Gospel should ever occupy the pulpit. Other speakers should stand to the side."

The minister at the church gave me very little guidance. "Speak on any topic you choose," he told me. "Just be sure you finish not later than ten minutes to twelve so we Methodists can beat the Baptists to the restaurant." That seemed to be a reasonable request, so I tailored my remarks accordingly.

I chose to speak on storytelling, on the importance and the joy of telling stories, especially family stories, to people we love. The talk went well. Members of the congregation were attentive and responsive, laughed at the right times and nodded in agreement every now and then. As I spoke my final words, I glanced at my watch. It showed eleven minutes to twelve. Perfect. With a smile to my listeners, I stepped back from the microphone, completely forgetting that I was in a raised pulpit. I instantly disappeared from view.

As I was falling, I heard a gasp from the congregation. I learned later that a few members thought it was the Rapture and I had been Received Up. They were, of course, strangers who did not know me well.

Rescuers rushed up. "Don't touch her!" one of the men in the vanguard ordered. "Don't touch her!" Though he meant to protect me, he sounded as if I had become an object of evil, a vile thing to be shunned. So I laughed. I lay there on the floor behind that raised pulpit in the Alabaster United Methodist Church and I laughed. I often laugh at inappropriate times.

My laughter should have been reassuring, but it had the opposite effect. "Oh, she must have a head injury!" one of the onlookers (nobody had dared touch me) exclaimed. He and other reasonable members of the group knew that only a person suffering from a mental disturbance would laugh at such a time.

I stopped laughing. "It's not my head," I assured them, "It's my shoulder that's hurt. My right shoulder." My diagnosis prompted strong hands to help me get up off the floor and guide me out to the parking lot where a waiting driver sped me to the emergency room of the Shelby Medical Center.

"How did the accident happen?" the efficient admitting clerk asked.

"She fell out of the pulpit," my escort replied.

"She fell out of the pulpit?" The clerk burst into laughter. "This woman fell out of the pulpit!" she announced to the assemblage of sick and injured patients huddled in the emergency waiting room. They, most of them, joined in the laughter. Two or three of them got up out of their plastic chairs and came to ask for details about my accident. Others just stared.

By then the gurney with its attendant had arrived to wheel me off to X-ray. Halfway down the hall, an earnest young intern stopped us to ask about my injury. He, too, inquired how the accident happened, and he, too, thought falling out of a pulpit was funny. He tried to hold on to his serious, professional manner, but he could not. He ducked quickly under the gurney where I could hear his muffled laughter.

It's all right," I told him. "You can laugh. Everybody else has." So he did.

The X-rays showed that I had a broken shoulder, not a painful injury, but a very inconvenient one. During my weeks of healing, I got awfully tired of hearing remarks about falling from grace and pride going before a fall.

Months later, after I was completely well, I was invited to speak at a banquet at an Air Force base in Colorado. All my friends helped me get ready for that trip: they wanted me to look my very best. Actually, their major concern was that I present a favorable image of Selma. I don't suppose we Selmians will ever stop being on the defensive about our home town, will ever stop trying to rebuild a good reputation for Selma. Our sad crusade is doomed to go on endlessly unless TV networks stop showing reruns of that shameful confrontation of civil rights marchers and billy-swinging mounted lawmen on our graceful river bridge.

So there I was, all dressed up in a lot of borrowed finery, my hair neatly arranged, my makeup on straight, standing in the foyer of the Officers' Club out in Colorado Springs, a long way from home. I was surrounded by a large cluster of high-ranking officers, including a few generals and their wives, and I was doing an excellent job of representing Selma well. Never have I felt more poised, more charming. I was about as near perfection as I ever expect to be. I wasn't sure how much I was actually helping Selma's image, but I was mighty pleased with my own. Then, in the midst of my bright, sophisticated conversation (I was using my best Southern accent) a young woman suddenly came out from the edge of the crowd and said in a loud voice, "Mrs. Windham, my mama saw you fall out of the pulpit in Alabaster!"

So much for creating positive images.

The second time I had a fall was a private occurrence, right in my own back yard. I was mowing the grass, what grass there is, and somehow in turning the mower around, I lost my balance, put out my hand to cushion my fall, and shattered my right wrist. Nothing spectacular, just pure clumsiness.

"You had no business mowing your yard," my wise friends told me. "You're too old for that." I had just turned seventy-four.

Maybe I am too old, but I like to cut the grass in my yards. They're small areas, just the right size for me to manage, and I do usually use an electric mower, a concession to my aged condition. The electric mower starts with the flip of a switch, is easy to guide, and I don't have to worry about keeping a supply of gasoline on hand. I do have to worry about keeping the long electric cord out of the path of the mower's blade. There are habitual predictors of calamity among my acquaintances who expect me to hack up at least two or three cords per season, but thus far I have disappointed them.

In case I should put the electric machine out of commission, I have a backup in the garage, a plain, old-fashioned push mower. I get it out and use it every now and then just because I like it. The job takes longer with a push mower, but it gives me time to think. I like the reassuring, wholesome, whirring sound it makes when I push and pull it across the yard. I like the arcs of fresh-cut grass its blades toss up. I like watching those blades turn over and over. I like being in complete control: the mower moves when I push, goes where I guide it, stops when I want it to. My decisions, my energy, my strength govern its behavior completely.

I like my push mower, too, because it attracts attention. Summer afternoons when I am propelling the mower back and forth across the front yard, boys on bicycles stop to see the human-powered marvel at work. Young mothers pushing babies in strollers pause to watch. Older couples interrupt their strolls to reminisce about "the good old days" and to comment about how "they don't make things like they used to."

Occasionally one of the spectators asks, rather hesitantly, "Could I try it?" Feeling a close kinship to Tom Sawyer, and with a proper show of reluctance, I grant that privilege. Some afternoons I get half the front yard cut that way.

So, as soon as my doctor removed the bandages and extracted the four metal pins from my wrist, I got my trusty mower out and cut the grass. I hope I can cut grass and rake leaves (I don't much like to bag them) until I die.

When I rake leaves, I collect them first in an old cotton basket, one Lige Danzy wove from oak splits a long, long time ago.

I have a photograph of Lige, barefooted and smiling, weaving a basket on the front porch of his house. I'd like to think he was making the basket I have now, but I know he wasn't. My basket was made in our back yard in Thomasville on one of those days when Lige appeared at our kitchen door with a bundle of splits balanced on his shoulder.

"Tell Miss Helen I'm here to put new bottoms in the porch rockers and make her a new clothes basket and whatever else she wants made," Lige said to Thurza, our cook. "And put a little more sugar in my coffee 'fo you go," he added. Lige always drank a cup of Thurza's strong, hot coffee before he started work.

He usually worked in the shade of a big chinaberry tree in the back yard, the tree whose brittle limbs held my treehouse. Actually it was not a real treehouse, just a sideless platform of boards, but it was my retreat. Lige sang and talked to me while he bottomed the chairs and wove the baskets.

"Somebody fat, bigger than me, been settin' in this chair. You been settin' in it?" he teased. "Near 'bout done set the bottom plum' out! Good thing I come today. May need to have another cup of Miss Thurza's good coffee so I can fix it right."

I relayed his request to Thurza, and she, with laughing banter, suggested that Lige's wife should learn to make good coffee. I was quite willing to bring Lige as many cups of coffee–each one with extra sugar added–as he asked for. I kept hoping he would teach me to weave a basket.

"Ain't no need for you to learn," he told me in answer to my pleas for a lesson. "Some folks can make good baskets and some can't. I can. Always was quick and apt about making baskets. You learn to do something else. This big old basket I'm making for your mama now will last you all your life. It will be here when you're a old lady, older even than me."

I laughed at the absurdity of ever getting as old as Lige, ever getting to be "a old lady."

But I have. And Lige's basket is still in use.

That basket has not been in my possession all those years. In fact, I had not even thought about that basket for more than half a century. One morning I had a call from Thomasville from a young couple who rented the house I inherited from my cousin, Tabb Forster. "We've been clearing out the storage room back of the garage," they told me, "and we found some things we think you might want to have."

So I drove down to Thomasville to see what they had found. Most of what they had salvaged was junk, stuff that needed to be thrown away, but in the midst of it all was Lige's basket. It was dirty and a little warped, but it was sound. For just an instant, I heard Lige's deep laugh and heard him say, "See? I told you so!" I brought the basket back to Selma with me and have used it ever since. One of the splits in the bottom has broken, but it still holds leaves well, mighty well.

I don't know how many years Lige's basket spent in that storage room. It could have been put there in the mid-1930s when Mother and I moved in with Aunt Bet and Tabb. The mortgage on the house I grew up in had been foreclosed after my father's death, nearly all our furniture was sold, and Aunt Bet and Tabb took us in, just as Daddy and Mother had taken them into our home many years earlier. I'm grateful to whoever saved that basket for me as part of my inheritance after Tabb's death. I'll care for it and use it as long as I live.

The basket is certainly easier to care for than is the house Tabb left me. If I had any business sense at all, I would have sold that house and lot in the early 1980s, soon after Tabb died. Though I've never had difficulty renting it, repairs and insurance and taxes always cost me more than the rent brings. Just last summer, I spent roughly four times as much on renovating the house as it cost to build it.

Of course I should sell it. But I can't. How could I sell a home still inhabited by happy memories of people I loved? I walk through the rooms and I see their faces, hear their voices: Aunt Bet, Tabb, Mother, Annelee, Amasa, Sister Edith, Thurza, Mymie, Ida, Heather, all whispering to me, "Do you remember? Do you remember?"

Nor can I sell Tabb's car. Her 1971 green Plymouth Valiant sits in my driveway now. Its slant-six engine performs perfectly, but it does need cosmetic attention: the paint (I have had it repainted once) is cracking, the vinyl upholstery has burst open in spots, the windshield has cracks in it, the speedometer doesn't work, the rubber gaskets around the doors and windows have rotted. But it runs great. Tabb had driven it almost ten years when it came into my possession, and it had only ten thousand miles on it. Since I've had it, the odometer registered well over one hundred thousand miles before it quit keeping score. I forgot to mention that the windshield wiper does not work and that the car has no air-conditioning. It lacks power steering, too. Tabb never saw much sense in spending money on such luxuries as air-conditioning and power steering.

My children call my Valiant all manner of unflattering names and refuse to drive it or to ride in it. Their opinions alter my affection for the car not one whit. I look on it as my pickup truck. Its trunk holds almost as much cargo as the bed of a small pickup holds, and the items I store there have the advantage of being protected from the weather and being securely locked. The back seat is where I store bundles of newspapers and sacks of beer cans until my collection gets even with the top of the front seat. Then I take the papers and the cans to the recycling centers. I always ask that the money from the sales of the cans be credited to the Church Street United Methodist Church, an act that tends to soothe my Methodist conscience.

One of these days when I'm affluent–or think I am–I'm going to have Tabb's car restored to mint condition. And I'm going to be very selective in choosing my passengers.

But back to my falls. My third fall was the worst of all, not because of its seriousness but because I was so far from home. It happened in Berlin in December 1992. I tried to make a good story of it by saying that I was carrying out a spy mission for the CIA and fell as I was scaling the Berlin Wall to safety. I even had an authentic piece of the wall to show to verify my story. But nobody believed me: All my listeners knew that the infamous wall had been torn down before I ever went to Germany. I never even saw the remains of the wall.

What really happened was that I failed to see a step in a poorly lit hall at an elementary school where I was telling stories, and I tumbled to the concrete floor. I was chatting with my bright fifth-grade hostesses instead of looking where I was going.

Jennifer (Mrs. Vernon) Miller, a fifth-grade teacher in the American school for military dependents (No, I was not telling stories in German!) had arranged for me to spend a week at the school telling stories and encouraging pupils to write. I was amazed that my transportation and lodging would be paid for in addition to a generous honorarium. Until I had a fall at midweek, it was one of the most exciting vacations I ever had.

As soon as I hit the floor, I knew I had done serious damage to myself. I was able to get up off the floor unassisted, but I could not walk. My two escorts were crying (I was not crying—I seldom do) and actually wringing their hands until I dispatched them to go get Jennifer and the school nurse. Jennifer was more upset and frightened than her pupils were, but, thank God, she did not cry. She and the nurse, a stalwart woman, got me into a wheelchair from which I was eventually transferred to an ambulance and carted off to the U. S. Military Hospital in Berlin.

German doctors examined me in the emergency room and ordered me admitted to the hospital. The doctors spoke flawless English. The only German words I knew were Guten Morgen (Good Morning), but it was afternoon so I could not use them. I felt very stupid. I also felt very, very uncomfortable.

Soon after I was settled in my hospital bed, the assistant administrator came in to see me.

"I was born in Selma, Alabama," he told me, "and when I saw

someone from Selma on the patient list, I wanted to come meet you." He was a very personable man. His family lived in Selma only a few months after his birth (he did return once as an adult to seek out the hospital where he was born), but he felt a certain responsibility for a patient from his natal city. How fortunate and how grateful I was! Not only did I have excellent nursing service (I never waited longer than three minutes between the time I pressed the button for a nurse and the time a nurse appeared), my ex-Selma friend brought me German chocolates, lotion and newspapers from Alabama.

When, after three days in the hospital, I finally was able to get a flight home, he volunteered to take me to the airport in his van.

"I know you have not had time to do much sight-seeing in Berlin," he told me, "so I'll come early to pick you up and will give you a brief tour of the city, if you feel like it." I accepted his offer gladly.

On the morning of my departure, he arrived promptly, ready to be my tour guide. Unfortunately, I discovered that I was too incapacitated to get on the seat in the van. I had to slide across the floor behind the front seat and sit there with my crutches beside my outstretched legs.

He did take me on a tour of Berlin, pointing out statues and buildings and historic sites. The only trouble was, I could not see what he was talking about: from my position on the floor, all I could see were the tops of trees and the roofs of buildings. He took so much pleasure in providing this tour for me that I did not want him to know I could not see what he thought he was showing me. I tried hard to make appropriate comments. I hope I did.

The plane trip home was not the ordeal I had feared. If I sat perfectly still, there was no pain. So I sat perfectly still from Berlin to Atlanta, from Atlanta to Montgomery and then by car from Montgomery to Selma.

My Selma doctor found I had broken my pelvis in two places. In due time I graduated from bed rest to walker to cane. I was free of pain but had a slight limp, what my brother Wood always spoke of as a "distinguished limp." Even that soon disappeared.

Truth is, I seldom even think about my falls unless somebody brings the subject up. When I asked my doctor if I had bad bones and he replied, "No, you just have bad luck," I was greatly relieved. I could even erase the memories (almost) if people would stop asking me, "Fallen out of any pulpits recently?"

However, there are other reminders of the vicissitudes of aging. Before I get out of bed each morning, I have to do knee-to-chest exercises to strengthen my back, put drops in my eyes to prevent glaucoma, and pull on heavy support hose or socks to hold varicose veins at bay. I remember when my doctor first ordered me to wear that unattractive hosiery, my daughter Kitti, who always looks on the bright side of any situation, told me, "Well, those socks and stockings aren't all that ugly. And just think–you'll never have to shave your legs again!"

After breakfast, there are pills and capsules to take to medicate my ailing heart, and sometime during the day I am supposed to walk at least a mile. I have walked almost daily for a quarter of a century, which is one reason I was surprised when I developed what is generally referred to as heart trouble. I like to walk, but something in me rebels at walking circle after circle around the track at the athletic field, or at pacing past the stores inside the mall. I feel compelled to combine my exercise with a worthwhile errand: mailing letters at the post box seven blocks away, taking clippings or written pages to Williams Photographic to be copied, going to Wal-Mart to buy gem clips or flashlight batteries or bird food or such.

I remember one summer afternoon when I had been digging in a flower bed in the back yard, I decided to take my walk. I was disheveled and had on grubby clothes, but it never occurred to me to spruce up for

Lest anyone think I'm not keeping fit, here I am with my dukes up at my favorite exercise salon.

my delayed exercise. My route took me by a home where one of the neighbors' daughters, Ruth, was playing in the yard with a child I did not know.

"Hello, Ruth," I said, not breaking my stride.

"Hello, Mrs. Windham," Ruth replied.

Then I heard the visiting child say, "That's not Mrs. Windham," to which Ruth replied, "It certainly is!" Her playmate said with disbelief, "That can't be Mrs. Windham: she wouldn't look like that." Ruth declared, "It is Mrs. Windham. She's my friend, and I've seen her look a lot worse!"

I'm glad I slowed my pace enough to hear that exchange. I laughed to myself all the way home.

Somehow I had thought that my habit of walking plus what I considered reasonable concern for my diet would protect me from heart problems, and they did until I was nearly seventy-five. I have a notion that we're living a lot longer than God intended for us to live–but I'm not eager for Him to revert to His original plan, not quite yet. I sometimes feel greedy, and a bit guilty, when my son, Ben, reminds me teasingly, "Remember, you've used up your allotted time of three score years and ten. You're living on borrowed time!"

Yearly physical checkups have also been a part of "taking care of myself," as I'm urged to do. However, it was on an unscheduled visit (I had gone to ask about a small lump on my lip which, strangely, shrank away while I was in the waiting room) that a casual remark I made to the doctor about brief episodes of having felt light-headed and giddy set off a series of examinations and tests of my heart. When the results were analyzed, a specialist explained to me that I had a very irregular heart beat, sometimes dropping to thirty beats per minute and occasionally skipping beats entirely.

"You must have a pacemaker," he told me. "You should have it done as soon as we make arrangements with the surgeon and the hospital."

I protested, telling him that the procedure would have to be postponed for a few days. "I'm going down to Gulf Shores tomorrow to join all my family for a long weekend to celebrate my birthday."

He looked straight at me and said, "There may be nothing to celebrate."

So I spent my seventy-fifth birthday in the Selma Medical Center having a pacemaker installed. I thought perhaps somebody in the operating room would sing "Happy Birthday," but nobody did.

I did hear it sung with love and fervor, if not much harmony, the next day when I joined my family at Gulf Shores at a house, a big house, right on the beach.

My grandsons (one was two and one was five) and I waded along the edge of the water, laughing when waves played tag with us. We watched sand crabs scurry sideways to their homes, collected shells, built frog houses instead of fancy castles, printed our names in the damp sand, sang silly songs, told stories, pretended we could fly like the gulls, and laughed some more. Sometimes we let the adults play with us.

It was the most wonderful, the most truly wonderful, birthday I ever had. Except to be grateful for it, I was never aware of the silver-dollar-sized miracle implanted near my heart.

My Friend Fred

It had been a long time since I had thought of my friend Fred, Fred J. Eldridge, and if I had not taken a sudden and rare notion to straighten up my living quarters, there's no telling when he would ever have come to mind.

The anticipated arrival of company prodded me into cleaning up one recent weekend. I had no hope of impressing my guests with my housekeeping (they know me rather well), but I did feel it necessary to have places for them to sit. All the chairs in the part of the house where we would normally congregate were serving as temporary filing areas for unread magazines, clippings, letters both answered and unanswered, books, notes for writing-in-progress, photographs, my grandsons' toys, stacks of clothes destined for Goodwill and other such impediments to sitting.

I went to the garage where I store boxes to use in just such emergencies, and I found several containers exactly the size I needed, the size that fits under beds. It was only after I had relieved the chairs of their burdens and had stuffed the clutter into the boxes that I made a terrible discovery: there was no room under any bed for even one more box! My strong inclinations to keep things, my sentimentality, my indecisiveness, my tendency to start collections, my procrastination, and, yes, my forgetfulness finally made it necessary for me to take unaccustomed action: I would have to throw away the contents of some of the boxes that had for too long lurked under my beds.

Opening those boxes and looking inside was a mistake, a delaying tactic, too, perhaps, but I had to do it. I kept hoping I would come across some long-lost treasure, such as my son's collection of baseball cards (he never comes home without asking me if I've found them yet, as though I am solely responsible for their disappearance), but I did not. I found mail-order Christmas presents intended for giving four or five years ago; research on the life of Julia Tutwiler; copies of weekly newspaper columns I wrote decades ago when the children were growing up; old photographs and negatives; souvenirs from the summer (1962) we spent in Greece, Italy and Turkey; epitaphs, pictures and stories from old graveyards. That's only a partial inventory. Obviously there was nothing I could discard.

I was pondering possible rearrangement (I had already filled the trunk of the car with must-be-preserved boxes: car trunks are grand temporary storage places as are stove ovens) when I raked from the farthest recesses beneath a double bed not a box but a basket, a market basket made of white oak splits. It was filled with letters. I chuckled as I read the return address on the top letter: Fred J. Eldridge—World's Greatest Writer—VA Hospital—Tuskegee, Alabama. I looked at those envelopes, more than two hundred of them, holding Fred's letters, stories, poems, drawings and songs, and I wondered why I had kept them for over a quarter of a century.

My interest in Fred's writings began when I was still working as a reporter for the *Selma Times-Journal.* One morning while conferring with the editor, Roswell Falkenberry, in his office, I chanced to glance at his wastebasket and was attracted by an envelope addressed in large, bold writing. When I inquired about it, the editor told me, "Oh, we get one or two fat letters a week from that fellow. He's a patient at the Veteran's Hospital in Tuskegee. Used to live in Selma, I think. We just throw the stuff away." I retrieved the envelope and read its contents.

From then on, I made certain that Fred's correspondence came to my desk. I sent him a supply of copy paper (no longer a staple in newspaper offices) and several pencils, and before long the envelopes with his distinctive handwriting began to be addressed to Editor K. Windham. Some of my newspaper friends still call me Editor K.

Fred wrote long, imaginative stories, printing each chapter or installment in pencil. His spelling was unbelievably awful, and his punctuation was quite peculiar: he either put a period after each word, or he used no punctuation or capitals at all, or he put a period at the end of each line. Sometimes he numbered the lines in the left-hand margin. Always across the top of page one he identified himself, printed the name of his composition and dated it. He was very particular about dates.

I picked one of the envelopes out of the basket, brushed off a silverfish and began to read. I wanted to be sure my memories of Fred's writings were accurate before I decided how to dispose of them. The envelope I had chosen contained an installment of a long story about Judge Sam Rights and his courtroom adventures. When I had finished reading it, I was eager to search through the basket for the other chapters. Even with his strange punctuation and misspelled words, Fred's story was as readable, intriguing and fresh as when I first chanced upon his writings. Again I was impressed by his enjoyment of words and by his sense of humor, reflected even in his choices of names: Dr. Will Doright, Lawyer Jes Intime, Moviemaker James Oversize, The Longhair Barber Shop, Lawyer Buck Goodgravy, The Paymore Hospital and others.

I plucked out another envelope. In it were two church songs, according to Fred's identification across the top of each page. One song was called "Jesus Gave Me My Light" and the other was titled "He Can't

Fred Eldridge with his typewriter, a gift from Selma Mayor Joe T. Smitherman.

Go To Church No More Cause He Wink At The Deacon's Daughter," and they were as different as their names indicate.

Straightening up the house was forgotten as I indulged myself in the pleasure of rediscovering the writings of my friend Fred Jackson Eldridge.

We met only once. My friend Fred and I met in Tuskegee when I went over to the hospital to take him a typewriter. On the back of one of his manuscripts he had printed, "I could write better if I had me a typewriter. A used one would do." So I scrounged around to get a typewriter for Fred. To be truthful, it was Mayor Joe Smitherman who did the scrounging and found a used but sturdy Underwood upright, just right for Fred.

Two of my children, Dilcy and Ben, rode over to Tuskegee with me to deliver the machine to Fred. I had informed him of our planned visit, though I had not told him of its purpose, and he was waiting for us in the visitors' area of the hospital when we arrived. He was a middle-aged man, stocky and balding, with a pleasant, gracious manner. He wore a nicely pressed suit, white shirt and dark tie instead of the hospital garb I had somehow expected. He looked like a teacher or a preacher. Maybe even a successful writer.

When Ben brought the typewriter in from the car and deposited it on a nearby table, Fred broke into a grin. "Mine?" he asked. "Yours," I replied. "Mayor Smitherman sent it to you." His grin widened. He needed some help to roll a sheet of copy paper (we took him a big batch) into the carriage, making me wonder if he had ever used a typewriter before. But once the paper was in place, he began to peck out his name and the date across the top of the page.

"You're ready to write now," I commented. "No telling how many stories you will type."

"No telling," he replied. "I do like to write. Sometimes I get started and it seems like I can't write fast enough to put down the stories that just keep hurrying through my head. I write for two or three hours at a time sometimes, and I hate to stop." His glasses had a tendency to slip down on his nose, and he pushed them back in place with what seemed to be a nervous habit.

"You wrote a long story about Bill Split and his rich old mule," I said. "I liked that story."

"I liked it, too," Fred replied. We laughed together as we recalled the funny predicaments Bill Split's mule got him into. "I hated for that story to end." He pushed his glasses up and was silent for a moment. "Of course," he said, "I could keep on writing that story. All I'd have to do is erase 'The End' and just write some more."

And he did. He wrote scores and scores of "literaries" as he called them. I do not understand what prompted his desire, even his compulsion, to write any more than I understand why I saved his notes and his manuscripts. I do know that he, as do all writers, longed to see his stories in print, and I know, too, that he hoped some day to become rich and famous.

As I sat there rereading some of his compositions, choosing them at random from the basket, I was touched by the instructions he gave for handling the royalties he hoped to receive, by the generous spirit he possessed. Printed on the backs of pages were requests that royalties be distributed to such beneficiaries as the Wilby Picture Show so all children in Selma and Dallas County can go to the movies every Saturday; his mother and two of his daughters; Mt. Meigs Reform School to buy ice cream and candy for the boys every Saturday and Sunday; all the churches of Selma to help pay their light bills; Selma Street Department to pave all streets and sidewalks in Selma; Fred himself so he could put his suit and shirt in the cleaners and get a haircut and get his shoes shined to go to church clean on Sundays; my son, Ben Windham, so he could have a guitar band of his own; the Red Cross for all the crippled people in Selma; a fund to construct a building for "peoples who don't have no where to sleep and eat and can't work and don't have no money at all and just living with kin folks and kin folks is not able to worry with the person–then they can live in my building free!"; and the U. S. War Department to help President Johnson win the war in Vietnam. That's just a partial listing of how Fred would use his royalties, royalties he never earned.

Thinking back over the years I received those envelopes addressed to Editor K., I realized how little I really know about Fred's personal life. At our one meeting, I learned that he had been a cook in the Navy during World War II, and that he had been a patient in the VA Hospital for about fifteen years. "I'm not crazy," he assured me, but I never learned what his problem was. The thought of that building he wanted to construct for "peoples whose kinfolks are not able to worry with them" kept creeping into my mind.

I did know, because he told me so, that Fred was a fine cook, was proud of his cooking. In addition to cooking in the Navy, he had been a cook for the diner on a passenger train. "I had to cook and to jump," he told me. "There was just a little bitty space around the stove, and if you brushed against that hot stove, you had to jump!" He laughed at the memory. He talked with pride about cooking four steaks for Jeanette McDonald ("the singing movie star" he identified her) when she sang at the Wilby Theatre in Selma in 1939. Fred was cooking then at the Splendid Cafe, located between the Wilby and the Hotel Albert where Miss McDonald was staying. She summoned him out of the kitchen to tell him he was the best steak cook in the whole USA, Fred told me.

Later I learned that Fred had worked awhile for Circuit Judge Thomas Knight on Tremont Street in Selma. It must have been through his association with Judge Knight that Fred became familiar with the courtroom scenes and legal procedures that he wove so authentically into his stories. It could have been that Fred himself was involved in trials and difficulties with the law such as he wrote about. I don't know.

Because of his expertise in cooking steaks, Fred applied for a job as cook on President Lyndon B. Johnson's Texas ranch. Somewhere in that basket is a copy of his application. "I don't need to look in no cookbook," he wrote. "I no cooking by hard."

Although he did not get the job as cook, Fred considered the President his personal friend. One of his treasures was a "gold" Christmas card from President Johnson who, Fred wrote me, sent an FBI man to make sure Fred received the gold greeting.

Somewhere in that basket are Fred's accounts of sending copies of his "literaries" to people of prominence throughout the world including President Harry Truman, Dean Martin, England's Queen Elizabeth, President Dwight Eisenhower, Hugh Downs of the Today show, mayors of the nation's largest cities, President Richard Nixon, President Charles deGaulle of France, and no telling how many others. He felt a close kinship with President Nixon because they were both born in 1913, which, Fred said, made them good friends. President Nixon sent him a Christmas card with a picture of the Nixon family as affirmation of their close ties, he pointed out.

There's a copy of a letter Fred wrote to "My Dear Good Friend President Richard Nixon" suggesting that the two of them go to France on June 23, 1969, and spend a month with President deGaulle. Fred was eager to show his good friend, President Charles deGaulle, how to cook steaks and how he types his Christmas songs. He had earlier expressed a wish that Selma Mayor Joe Smitherman accompany him on his visit to deGaulle, but he apparently decided President Nixon would be a more desirable companion.

The idea for visiting the French head of state came after President deGaulle wrote Fred a note of thanks for sending him a Christmas composition. The note, sent air mail, came in an impressive official envelope embossed "President de la Republique." Fred sent me Xeroxed copies of the four-line note and of the envelope. I failed French in college, so I could not translate the handwritten message. This is what Fred wrote President Nixon about it: "Did President deGaulle tell you he sent me a xmas card and he wrote the xmas card in french writing why I could read some lines and could not make out the other two lines but I got a French man to read the other two lines to me and it read I thank you for the xmas song and I am sinding you a great gift for xmas day well its sure nice to say that President deGaulle like me so mutch because I sent him his first xmas gift in 1968 and he was glad to git my new song and he might have learn how to sang the xmas song now."

Reading those old letters from Fred, I keep being amazed at his feeling of intimacy with world leaders and at his enduring optimistic expectation that one of them would recognize his talents and reward him with the fame and fortune he knew he merited. And I keep wishing Fred and Joe Smitherman could have gone to France to visit the chief of state. They would have had such a good time, much better than Fred would have had if President Nixon had been his traveling companion. And what a trio they would have been, Fred, Joe and Charles, singing Fred's songs!

Fred's literary efforts did earn him some recognition. In 1968, I entered a sample of his writings in the National Hospitalized Veterans Writing Project contest, a contest that attracted thousands of entries. The judges awarded Fred two prizes, one for a resume of "The Book I'd Like to Write" and the other for the opening chapter in the book. I was pleased that Fred's entries won him cash awards, and I was greatly impressed when I learned that the judges in the category he entered were Margaret Cousins, senior editor for Doubleday and Co., and bestselling author Adela Rogers St. John.

Fred was not at all impressed by the judges, but he was mighty pleased by their decisions. He wrote me, "Now, Editor K. Windham, you told those government folks in Tuskegee, Alabama, about how good my story was about Bill Split and His Mule and they just smiled. They thought you was just joking, but now they know you was telling the truth about my story." That's the edited version of what he wrote. He credited President Eisenhower with entering his story in the contest: "This is the story what I sent to President Eisenhower for his birthday in 1967, and he mail it in and the story won two prizes in 1968. I, Fred J. Eldridge, will always love him for helping me win two prizes in 1968. Sure I will miss President Eisenhower. Who else will be that good to poor broke me but him and Mayor Joe T. Smitherman of Selma, Alabama, and I pray that God will let Mayor Smitherman live 80 more years because he is the only true friend I got left now in this world."

He did add a postscript (he never used just the two letters P.S. but always wrote P.S.T.) saying: "Now, I want to thank you Editor K. so mutch for what you did for poor me and God will let you live a long time on his earth. That will be your pay from God for helping poor me to be some one like all other good book writers in the U. S. A."

What more sincere thanks could I want?

It was soon after he was awarded prizes in the veterans' writing contest that Fred began adding "World's Greatest Writer" to his return address.

Fred loved Selma, wanted to come back here to live. Every now and then he would write about wanting to get enough money to buy back his white house with green trim on St. Ann Street that he sold for $300. "When I take one look at Selma Alabama it make my heart jump with joy," he wrote, "And when I meet somebody on the streets they say good morning Fred and they say hey there Fred how are you but up here don't no one say good morning to poor me and I can't get a good wife up here but I could get one every second in Selma."

Since he could not come to Selma to seek a wife, Fred sent me an ad to run in the *Selma Times-Journal.* He would like to marry, he wrote me, any brown or black woman in Selma who would marry him. In order to qualify, the prospective bride must be between twenty-five and thirty years old, weigh one hundred twenty or one hundred ten pounds and be able to cook diabetic food. He provided his telephone number and promised to marry the first woman who called. I decided against running the ad, and Fred never mentioned it again though he did comment months later that he still hoped to marry some good-looking woman "while I can still see good."

I was about to put all of Fred's literaries back in the basket (they should be arranged in chronological order!) when two bits of poetry slid into my lap. One of the poems expressed Fred's intention to fly up to Heaven to see if "Old Gabe" has sweet milk and honey there before Fred goes to stay, sort of checking out the accommodations. The other poem was titled "Wright From Wrong" and was a lament that his pretty baby drank too much wine on Christmas Day and ended up in the kitchen fast asleep with her feet in the ice box and a raw chicken wing in her mouth, all because she did not know "Wright From Wrong." I could almost hear Fred laughing as he wrote those poems.

Down in the bottom of the basket was a folder marked "Fred J. Eldridge Artis." I had forgotten about Fred's pictures. I spread them out, more than a dozen of them, to study them. There were monsters, churches, houses, a slice of watermelon, and elephants, some drawn with black, blue and red ink and some drawn with bright-colored crayons. They are pure folk art, just as his writings are.

Fred's art, both written and drawn, deserves to be published. As long as he lived, I tried to persuade publishers to put Fred's work in print, but although some of them showed interest, nobody was willing to take a chance on publishing what one editor called "interesting, fresh but too unorthodox for us to take on." Fred never gave up hope that his "literaries" would appear in print. He wrote me once, "I am down now, but some day the moon will shine in my face and I will have so mutch money that all the gin cotton houses won't be able to bale it up in ten years." So I kept all of Fred's artistic creations and kept hoping.

Then in 1976 Fred died. I know nothing about the details of his death, not even the exact date or where he is buried. I learned of Fred's death when I wrote to the VA hospital to express concern because I had heard nothing from Fred in several months. I was informed that Mr. Eldridge had died.

So I packed up those many envelopes, those pages and pages of stories and poems and songs that Fred had written. I had almost forgotten about them until that urge to clean up prompted me to drag out the containers under the beds.

New copyright laws make it virtually impossible for me to have his writings published–or even to publish them myself. The letters, according to the copyright laws, do not belong to me even though they were addressed to me and would have been lost forever if I had not saved them.

I know how to dispose of the other clutter under my beds. But what can I do with Fred?

Fred Eldridge wrote stories and songs, and he also drew many pictures. He especially liked to draw monsters.

Photography and Other Interests

My conscience troubles me that I have never thanked the Eastman Kodak Company for the Brownie they gave me back in 1930, the summer I was twelve years old. Perhaps it is not too late to thank them for the gift that introduced me to the world of photography, a hobby that has given me pleasure for more than sixty-five years.

I do not now recall how I first learned of Eastman's plan to give away thousands of box cameras to twelve-year-olds as part of the celebration of the company's fiftieth anniversary. I may have seen a notice in the window at People's Drug Company, the authorized Kodak dealer in Thomasville, or I may have read an advertisement in the Thomasville Times. I do recall that I was first in line the day those Brownies were distributed.

On the appointed day, I was up and dressed at daylight, and I ran down the hill, through the lumber yard and across the railroad tracks to the drugstore where I sat on the edge of the high sidewalk and waited more than an hour for Clayton Megginson to come open the store and start handing out the cameras. I doubt that People's Drug Company's allotment was large enough to meet the requests of all the local twelve-year-olds, but I did not sympathize with friends who were left out: they should have arrived on the scene earlier. I had my first camera. It was not fancy, but it was mine.

Sixty-three years later, I was informed that I was a Photographer with a capital P. In the intervening years, I had graduated from the Brownie to a folding Kodak with settings for lens openings and shutter speeds, to a cumbersome Speed Graphic to a Yashika (still my favorite) and finally to a Canon and a Pentax.

Through the years, I kept most of my negatives, even those I took as a reporter for the *Selma Times-Journal.* I wish I had kept all the negatives in the files there: when the newspaper was sold in the early 1970s, new personnel tossed the accumulation of decades of negatives into the Alabama River. My negatives were never filed in an orderly fashion, or in any fashion at all, but I did have them. Still do. I had prints made from a few of my favorites, and I hung them around the house. The ones that attract the most attention, six of them, are framed in a wooden window sash that I salvaged from a trash pile. To be honest, it is the framing and not the quality of the photographs that catches the eye of visitors.

It was not those sash-framed pictures that caught the eye of Frances Robb, however. Frances, one of the South's most knowledgeable persons in the field of both the historic and the artistic significance of photographs, had come to my house to inquire about the pictures John Reese had taken in Gee's Bend. We talked about John's photographs and about Gee's Bend, and I showed her quilts my friends there had made for me. As she was leaving, she paused to look at two framed photographs hanging on my dining room wall.

"Who took these?" she asked. When I told her that I was the photographer, she asked if I had any more. So I brought out an album of photos, and I showed her bags and boxes and drawers of negatives. She turned the pages of the album slowly, pausing every now and then to ask about the people or the landscape in the picture.

As she closed the album, she said matter-of-factly, "Your work must be exhibited. These are telling images."

I had never thought of my pictures as being "works," and it had certainly never occurred to me that they were worthy of being exhibited. I was still in a state of disbelief when twenty-eight of my photographs, each one printed with artistic feeling by Melissa Springer of Birmingham, were hung in the Huntsville Museum of Arts in late August 1993.

People, lots of dressed-up people, came to the opening night's festivities to wander through the gallery (I was lurking in the background watching and telling myself, "All these strangers have come to see your pictures"), to sit in the museum's theatre while I showed slides of the photographs and told stories about them, and, later, to mingle at an elegant reception.

Four of the photographs in the museum were made with my Brownie: my playmates Evelyn and Teace Cleiland about to take their first airplane ride; Hiram Davis, an ex-slave, in downtown Thomasville; Lige Danzy weaving a basket; and an old woman with a spinning wheel.

Since its premiere in Huntsville, my exhibit has traveled to the museum of Natural History in Anniston, the Birmingham Public Library and the University of Alabama in Tuscaloosa. I have taken the slide show, which is almost no trouble to set up, to the University of Montevallo, to Old Alabama Town in Montgomery and to the Selma-Dallas County Public Library, in addition to showing it at the opening of each of my photographic exhibitions.

I was especially proud to show the slides at the Selma library: it was the first program in the new Gerald Scrushy Learning Center after that addition opened in early February, 1995. Although I saw the plans develop and prayed fervently for funds to finance the project, watched the construction since the first stakes were connected by tight cords, and even applauded as a line of Gerald Scrushy's grandchildren cut the ribbons at the grand opening, I still can't quite believe the building is there. Every now and then I have to go to town and drive around the library block two or three times just to reassure myself that good dreams really do come true.

It seems such a short time ago Becky Nichols, the librarian, said to me, "I don't know what to do! We've run out of space in the library. I have to cram the children into a small upstairs area, and we don't have any place for young adults, and the genealogical section is overflowing, and adults need more room, and–"

"Go see the mayor," I advised her. For more than thirty years, Mayor Joe Smitherman has been the person to see about almost any project in Selma. Becky was hesitant, fearful that the mayor might not recognize the need for expanded library services. But she did go see Mayor Smitherman. He not only saw the limitations under which the library was operating, but he gave his enthusiastic support to plans for expansion. With his leadership, the City Council passed a bond issue to finance part of the construction costs, and the project was underway.

Contributions came from Selmians wishing to honor the memories of family members, from banks, utilities, local businesses, library users, schools, even children who emptied out their piggybanks. The largest single gift came from Richard Scrushy in honor of his father, for whom the facility is named.

No bequest touched me more deeply than did the $10,000 willed by Ernest Dawson, a black man from New York who grew up in Selma at a time when members of his race were not even permitted to enter the library.

Gifts such as that make it even more galling to me that the Dallas County Commission made not so much as a token gift, gave not a word of support to the project, nor have the members of the medical and legal communities, with few exceptions, seen fit to invest in the library.

I hope their consciences hurt every time they see that new building and every time their children and grandchildren find knowledge and pleasure there.

My two grandsons think the Scrushy Learning Center is wonderful. So do I.

There is another library in Selma, a much smaller library, in which I take pride. It is at Byrd Elementary School, a part of the Selma public school system, and it bears my name. The honor came to me unexpectedly, and it made me both happy and humble. Family members and friends assembled at Byrd for the dedication ceremonies on a hot summer Sunday afternoon in 1994. The occasion was a joyous one though it did give me the eerie feeling that I was eavesdropping on my own funeral.

My lifelong love of books is responsible for my devotion to libraries. The rambling frame house where I grew up in Thomasville was never painted, but there were books in every room. The first piece of furniture I ever owned as a child was a small oak bookstand. I still have it. Although I try to curb it, my collection of books continues to grow. When every bookcase is filled and the stacks of books on the floor begin to topple over, I put some of them in boxes and take them to the library. Parting with some of the volumes is difficult, but I tell myself they need to be discovered by new readers. No matter how crowded my bookcases are or how hazardous the towers of tomes become, I cannot part with my collections of books dealing with Alabama history, those by Southern writers, those on the subject of folklore or those autographed by the authors.

Books are not the only collections that clutter my house. My mother used to warn me, "Don't ever get more than two of anything or you'll find yourself collecting more than you want or know what to do with." How often I wish I had heeded her advice! My various collections give me pleasure, but they have tended to get out of hand.

There is, for example, my collection of insulators. I have no idea what attracted me to those glass objects that once were affixed to the cross-arms of utility poles, but after I learned about the different contours and colors and makes of insulators, I wanted more of them. My newspaper friend Nikki Davis Maute and I used to take croker sacks and walk old railroad roadbeds to find where poles had been cut down and insulators left where they fell. We would fill our sacks with as many as we could carry (each insulator weighs about a pound), bring them home and wash them in a tub in my back yard.

"What are you going to do with those things?" a curious neighbor asked one afternoon as I was washing some fine blue insulators with sharp drip points. She did not understand that you do not have to do anything with collections: the fun is in the collecting. However, she expected a logical answer, so I told her, "I'm going to make hummingbird houses out of them." She was satisfied with my reply.

I have lined flower beds with the insulators, inverted some and fitted them into hollowed-out wooden bases to use as pencil holders or vases, lined them up on sunny windowsills to catch the light, and given many of them away. But I still have more than a dozen metal garbage cans filled with insulators out in my garage. Be assured that I have quit actively collecting them, but people still bring me a few every now and then.

Then there is my collection of ghosts, not the wraiths themselves or even stories about them but ghostly figures created of ceramics, wax, wood, stained glass, cloth, metal, cake icing, clay and even cornshucks. I had no part in getting the collection. All I have done is to provide space, cramped though it is, for the gifts of ghosts that have come to Jeffrey and to me. A young guest recently counted ninety-seven ghostly figures in my house. Too many!

My collection of rabbits is smaller, but, as rabbits are said to do, it is multiplying. The rabbits, all shapes and sizes and materials of them, are the outgrowth of my involvement in the Rabbit Club. For more than a dozen years, a group of friends, all women, have met at a local restaurant at seven o'clock on the first day of each month for what we call Rabbit Breakfast. The gathering gets its name from an old superstition which promises that good luck will come to persons who yell out, "Rabbit!! Rabbit!!" as soon as they wake up and before they get out of bed on the first day of each month. We do not, as the name might suggest, eat rabbit for breakfast.

Our breakfasts are quite informal. Sometimes there'll be fifteen or sixteen diners present and sometimes there'll only be six or eight. Anybody who is in town, well, remembers to come and has the price of the meal is welcome. There are no membership rolls, no initiation fees, no dues and no minutes. We sit and talk, often all at the same time, and laugh a lot. Our only rule is that discussions of ailments and other doleful topics are banned.

The Rabbit Club, if such it can be termed, is the only social group with which I am affiliated. I am not a joiner.

My other collections almost defy explanation. What is there to say about boxes filled with dirt dauber nests (dirt daubers are fascinating and harmless insects) or clusters of old doorknobs or piles of driftwood from the coast or a score of blue glass objects, including an old Milk of Magnesia bottle, atop a filing cabinet?

I talked about my collections and about some of the pieces of furniture in the house on a videotape I gave each of my children one recent Christmas. They laughingly refer to it as "The House Not on The Tour of Historic Homes." I wanted to be sure they remember that the rocking chair in the den was made by Grandfather James Lee Tucker from a tree he cut on his Marengo County farm; that the small marble-top table in the living room was toted to safety on the two occasions that Grandmother Harriet Tabb's house burned; that the pine trestle table in the dining room is the first piece of furniture their daddy and I bought; that the armless rocker in the back bedroom is one of six applewood chairs, now scattered about my house, that the Tabbs brought from Virginia when the family moved to Alabama; that the long, heavy table I use as a writing desk came from my father's bank; and so forth.

Now I'm thinking of photographing pieces of furniture and bric-a-brac, writing a background story about each one and putting the pictures and the writing into albums, one for each child. I wish I had my Brownie to take the photographs with.

I really must thank Eastman Kodak.

Graveyards

I like graveyards. I do not like modern perpetual-care cemeteries with their rows of identical flat markers ("Makes it easier to mow, you know") and bunches of stiff plastic flowers on each grave. Call them "everlasting floral offerings" if you will; they are still ugly, those precise rows of identical vases holding their allotted numbers of artificial blossoms. When I ride past such burial places with their boring sameness, I grieve, grieve that surrender to uniformity has stripped the dead of their final vestiges of individuality.

On the rare occasions when I walk through such cemeteries, I find myself fearful and depressed, not by the thought of death but by the haunting dread that some strong force will overpower me, will snatch away my peculiarities and make me conform to the bland sameness of those neat graves. I hurry back to my car to escape from I know not exactly what.

In trying to sort out and catalogue my collections of photographs and negatives, a task I must complete, I find that though I have taken hundreds of pictures in graveyards, I do not have one single photograph taken in a perpetual-care cemetery. Nor have I ever found a good story in one.

Graveyards, on the other hand, abound with picture possibilities and with stories. I can spend hours wandering around in graveyards, reading the epitaphs, admiring the craftsmanship of the stonemasons, repeating the often lyrical names of the dead, grieving over the deaths of so many infants and young children, wishing I could hear the stories of the people buried there.

It is in those country graveyards that I find an affirmation and a celebration of our blessed differences, our divine differences, not only in life but in death. No two graves are alike, and even in the same family plots, the ways of honoring the dead may differ widely. There are still, far inland, in Southern graveyards, some mounded graves covered with seashells. As a child, I wanted to gather pocketfuls of those small shells and take them home with me, but Mother said, "Put them back. The woman buried there always wanted to see the gulf, but she never did. So after she died, her husband went to the coast and collected shells to decorate her grave."

I carefully replaced the shells I had taken, pressing each one into the ridged indentation where it had lain.

Now when I see other shell-covered graves (they are more and more rare) I wonder if they, too, are belated gifts to someone who never saw waves or a sandy beach or shore birds. Or shells.

In recent years I have found graves in old backwoods graveyards with less orthodox decorations: kerosene lamps, plates, cups, spoons, medicine bottles, broken boat paddles, warped Victrola records, even an old slop jar or two. The lamps, I was told, would light the dead on their journey into the other world. The plates, cups and spoons were used by the deceased to eat the last meal before death. The medicine bottles had held the final hope that the fatal illness might be cured. The boat paddles and records reflected the recreational choices of the departed. The slop jars? "They was needed," I was told.

A few of those graves once had iron bedsteads, the bed to which death came, to mark their head and feet, but thieves have carted those markers away. Other graves in those lonely locations were identified by hand-hewn wooden markers, thrust into the earth; markers the size and shape of a man's head and shoulders. The names and dates printed or scratched into the raw wood have been erased by time and weather, and many of the headboards themselves have rotted and collapsed.

Coming upon a cluster of those primitive wooden cutouts in an isolated, neglected burying ground is an eerie experience, not frightening, but rather like intruding on a gathering of a secret society whose members are following their ancestors' custom of stillness and of silence and of waiting. When first I happened upon such a scene, I hurriedly tiptoed away.

The strangest of these folk graveyards I have seen is the death mask burying ground at the Mount Nebo Baptist Church in lower Clarke County, down near the forks of the Alabama and Tombigbee Rivers. There a native craftsman, Ike Nettles, fashioned cement masks of his family and of friends and later affixed those masks to concrete markers on their graves.

When I first visited the Mount Nebo burials, back in 1974, a life-sized statue of a woman, a large woman, dominated the scene. Her long skirt touched the grass, and her arms were outstretched as though blessing the stone faces on the gravestones around her. It was, I was told, the figure of Selina Nettles, Ike's mother, a work he possibly considered his masterpiece.

When the statue was erected, soon after Selina's death in 1940, it had real hair, styled in the way Selina wore her hair, but the birds plucked out the strands to weave into their nests, and it was never replaced. Her arms were worn away by deer that came to scratch their backs on the rough surfaces. Time and nature have taken their toll on the figure, and it has collapsed, leaving only the cement mask intact.

Residents of the remote area recalled that the statue "looked just like Sister Selina." She was a large woman, they said, with a rump so big

A cement likeness of Sis Dollie is among the deathmasks fashioned by Ike Nettles. His art work was affixed to handmade grave markers at Mt. Nebo Church in a remote area of Clarke County.

she could set a five-gallon bucket of water on it and walk a mile without spilling a drop.

Nobody seemed to know how Ike got the idea for making death masks or where he learned the technique. The masks were fashioned while the subjects were still alive. Some reports say that they pressed their faces into a box of damp sand and Ike made his molds from those impressions. Other witnesses recalled that he used fine wire and strips of wet paper ("he put hollow straws up their noses so they could get their breath") to capture the facial contours. After the cement had hardened, he put the mask away until time came to affix it to the deceased's handmade concrete grave marker.

One of these upright markers bears three faces, the likeness of Ike's wife, Cora, and of their two daughters, Clara and Pollene. Nearby are the masks of his kinswoman, Esella "Sis Dollie" Nettles, with "Angel" spelled out in raised letters beside her face, and the mask-embellished tombstone of Manual Burell, who died in 1946.

Why did Ike Nettles make those masks? Some people say he made them because if God saw the faces of the deceased, He would recognize them and they would get to heaven faster. Another, more logical, theory is that the residents of the area had no money to spend on commercially made grave markers so they turned to Ike, one of their own, to create a fitting memorial for them.

If the unusual statuary in the Mount Nebo graveyard was appreciated and cherished by the congregation there, the same cannot be said for a statue in another Alabama churchyard, many miles away. There the life-sized likeness of a prosperous planter stirred up such a controversy that it almost split the church. Maybe it did. Details are a bit vague.

What is known is that the preacher and a majority of the deacons declared the statue to be a graven image and therefore unfit, sinful even, to be put at the deceased man's grave. Many bitter words and hard feelings later, it was decreed that the stone likeness could lie atop the grave. Standing, it was a graven image. Reclining, it was not.

The fine line of violation of the Second Commandment between an upright statue and a prone one was never fully clarified to the satisfaction of a goodly number of church members, the widow among them. However, after the passage of time, the church's leaders become more lenient in their interpretation of The Word and permitted the statue to be hoisted to an upright position at the head of the man's grave.

So he stands there even today in all his finery: frock tail coat, watch chain draped across his ample paunch, cane in hand and top hat on his head, looking not like a graven image but like the influential, admired personage he had always yearned to be.

Other fine pieces of funerary art, each with its distinctive history, summon me to many graveyards. Who can fail to be touched by the story and the statue of three-year-old Opal June Davis in a burial plot in suburban Birmingham? The little girl, clutching pennies in her chubby hand, was running down the sidewalk to the corner grocery store to buy candy when she darted into the street and was killed by an automobile. It was a June day in 1924.

The statue on her grave shows a wistful child with her blonde hair cut short. Her feet are bare as a carefree youngster's should be on a summer day in Alabama. One hand is pressed against her face, and the other hand is outstretched.

Soon after the statue was erected, visitors began putting pennies in June Opal's hand, a custom that continues to this day, more than seventy years after her death.

June Opal's pennies go to the Crippled Children's Clinic in Birmingham, gifts in memory of a child who died holding a handful of pennies.

Another child, a little girl only a year older than June Opal, has her memory kept alive by a brick playhouse erected over her grave in Lanett, Alabama.

Nadine Earles, the story goes, loved dolls. Her one desire was to have a doll house, one big enough for her and her friends to play inside with all her dolls.

"I know Santa Claus will bring you a doll house for Christmas," her father assured her when she begged him for the little house. Julian Comer Earles had already made arrangements to have the structure built.

But Nadine never got her wish: she died of diphtheria a week before Christmas in 1933.

Soon after Nadine's funeral, her father began building a doll house over the child's grave. "I promised Little Nadine a doll house, and she will have it!" he declared.

The house was finished by April 3, 1934, Nadine's fifth birthday. On that date, Mr. and Mrs. Earles invited the members of her Sunday School class to come to a birthday party at Nadine's doll house. It was a strange setting for a party, but the children, too young to be ensnared by melancholy, ignored the gloomy symbols of death that surrounded them as they played games, laughed, ate ice cream and cake and peeped through the windows of a small brick house at the dolls and toys of a friend they had already half forgotten.

Burying grounds abound with stories, so many stories!

There are, for instance, in Clayton, Alabama, the whiskey bottle tombstones, a large bottle-shaped stone at the head and a smaller one at the foot of the grave of William T. Mullen (1834–1863). His wife, a militant foe of whiskey, repeatedly vowed that if he did not quit drinking, she would mark his grave with granite replicas of the bottles that caused his moral and physical downfall. He didn't, and she did.

And there is the Coon Dog Memorial Graveyard in Colbert County, Alabama, restricted to the burial of coon dogs, where former owners of the deceased hounds gather each Labor Day to clean off the graves, eat barbecue and tell some of the South's finest hunting stories; a moss-draped South Alabama graveyard where a stone inscribed "IDA" marked the burial spot of a chubby toddler, who, the story goes, was eaten by her cannibal nurse while her parents attended a dance at a neighboring plantation; an isolated family burying ground near the Alabama River where lie three children shot by their father when he learned of General Robert E. Lee's surrender at Appomattox; the man and his wife both buried standing upright, he with a bottle of corn liquor in one hand and a butcher knife in the other, and she holding a broom, so they can meet in Hell and continue their earthly battles; the big crimson arrows painted on the winding pavement at Elmwood Cemetery in Birmingham to guide football fans to the final resting place of Coach Bear Bryant; an unmarked grave between two large mounds, said to be where a Clarke County resident was interred (at his written request there were no religious rites) between his two mules named The Lord and Jesus Christ; and hundreds, hundreds more.

So, is it any wonder that I, a storyteller, am attracted–addicted even–to wandering around in graveyards? Albums and boxes overflow with photographs of exquisite, intricate stonework, of unusual markers, of peaceful burial sites. Notebooks are filled with epitaphs, some in unmetered rhyme, some unimaginative and repetitious, some extolling at length the virtues of the deceased, some beautifully plain. The simple inscriptions touch me most deeply: "So Many Hopes Lie Buried Here" on the tombstone of a sixteen-year-old girl; or "She Made Our Home Happy" carved beneath the name of a middle-aged woman.

No burying ground lures me more often to stroll in it than does the Old Live Oak Cemetery here in Selma. When I am angry and frustrated by events over which I have no control, when I am smothered by feelings of insecurity and loneliness, or when my thoughts become entangled in thickets of confusion, I walk there, beneath the moss-draped branches of oaks and magnolias, to seek the peace and the strength I need. A strange simile perhaps, but those rows of old graves are as reassuring to me as are the waves on the beach at Gulf Shores, an unending affirmation of a Master Plan for all creation.

That graveyard was a favorite playing place for my children. On pleasant afternoons when they were very young, their nurse, Viola, would walk with them down Dallas Avenue to the walled burying grounds where the four of them joined other nurses with their charges. While the children played games of hiding, chase or tag among the tombstones ("Don't get too loud now–we don't want to bother the dead," they were admonished), the nurses sat along the low brick copings that bounded the family plots, talking and laughing softly until the lengthening shadows of grave markers reminded them to call the children from play and turn toward home.

Occasionally I picnic with friends at Old Live Oak. We roam a bit, pausing to comment on unusual tombstones or to tell stories about the deceased whose graves we recognize, before we select a spot to spread our lunch.

"Which family will be our hosts today?" we ask. "Shall we dine at the graves of people we know or shall we have our lunch with strangers?"

It is not a simple decision. Sometimes our choice is dictated by the seating comfort: we favor low walls or raised flat markers. Often the shade or the sun influences our choice. If we remember the people interred at our chosen spot, we talk about them, maybe even direct a few remarks to them.

Although I visit the graves of strangers, I seldom go to the graves of my own family: my grandparents, my parents, my brothers and sisters, my husband. I do not take flowers on Easter or Christmas or anniversaries. I do not plant grass or tend shrubs on the family plots. Only recently have I begun to wonder about this seeming neglect of people I loved deeply. I think of my deceased family members often, even tell stories about them, but I feel no urge or obligation to go to their graves.

Years ago I heard my mother say, "You honor the dead by caring for the living whom they loved." I hope I have done that.

I used to be amused at my sister, Annelee, my last sibling to die, who, after she reached eighty, became almost obsessed with making her funeral plans. She lived in Thomasville, sixty-five miles from Selma, and she used to call me to come listen to and record her plans. "Please come down here," she'd say, "and bring an indelible pencil." I have not seen an indelible pencil in years, not since I was in grammar school, but I would select a writing implement and go.

Annelee kept her funeral plans in a notebook on the right hand side of the top drawer of her chest of drawers. She had the entire day of her burial planned in detail. She even had instructions as to which trays and platters were to be used for serving finger food ("I do not want a meal served–just finger food") and exactly where those containers were to be placed. She seldom made changes in those plans.

Her major changes were in the selection of her pallbearers. "Read me the list," she would say, and she would interrupt my reading with, "No. Take his name off. I don't think he takes good care of his dog," or "No, I'd rather have him directing traffic than serving as pallbearer," or "He's too feeble now," or "He hasn't even been to see me in months."

Next would come the task of choosing replacements. The procedure could take hours. Then, a few weeks later, I'd be summoned again to bring the indelible pencil to rework the list. It got to be a family joke.

And now I find myself doing something of the same thing. I drive

Country graveyards such as this all have stories, hundreds of stories surrounding them. A marker here for a sixteen-year-old girl says simply, "So many hopes lie buried here."

along stretches of interstate highways and entertain myself by asking, "Who do I want to tote my coffin?" The older I get, the shorter the list of potential pallbearers becomes.

My coffin is ready. For almost ten years it has been in the back of my garage, sitting on top of garbage cans filled with my collection of insulators. It's beautiful. My friend John Moss made it for me.

I've forgotten now what prompted me to visit a local funeral home. When I told the polite young man who greeted me that I wanted to select a coffin, he assumed that a family member or close friend had died and made appropriate consoling remarks.

"It's for me, the coffin is," I told him. He lost a bit of his professionalism just for a moment. Recovering, he directed me into the display room where dozens of coffins were open for inspection. He called them caskets. I kept calling them coffins. He was delicately hesitant to quote prices, but I insisted. I was appalled! I've sent children to college and even bought a house for less than what some of those coffins cost.

"Don't you have just a plain wooden box?" I asked. "Maybe a box one of these fine coffins was shipped in?"

Now it was his turn to be appalled. "Oh, that wouldn't do at all," he said. His voice quivered with shock at the idea of such cheapness, such a break with tradition, such disrespect for the dead.

"I believe it would," I replied, and I left.

That's when I called John Moss.

John Moss is a master craftsman, a man who handles wood with reverence ("God made it," he says) as he repairs family heirlooms or fashions furniture to be cherished by generations of owners. He taught for a long time at the community college in Selma, and I had taken several courses from him. He watched and encouraged me one quarter when I stripped four coats of paint, one of them pink, from an antique spool bed. I finally got all the paint off except for some spots on the

insides of the railings.

"I'm not going to get the rest of the paint off. It won't show. Nobody will ever know it's there," I told my instructor.

"You and I will know, Mrs. Windham," he replied. So I spent two more nights removing the paint.

When I got John Moss on the telephone, after my visit to the funeral home, I said, "John Moss, I'd like for you to make my coffin, please."

There was a long pause. "What did you say, Mrs. Windham?"

"I said I would like for you to make my coffin, please."

"I'd be honored," he replied.

My only instruction was that it be plain and be made of pine.

"I understand," he said. And he did.

He made my coffin from one hundred and fifty year old pine lumber he salvaged from a warehouse, and he put it together with walnut pegs. It is shaped in the old folk way, six-sided, wide at the shoulders and tapering to the feet. The handles (who will hold them?) are made of rope. The pine exterior has been sanded and rubbed to the smoothness of the worn arms of a long-used rocking chair.

The cost? Two hundred and fifty dollars.

When he delivered my coffin, bearing it proudly with the help of an equally proud apprentice, he told me, "There's a little sack of nails in here, Mrs. Windham, old square nails, to nail the top down. I didn't figure you would want to be viewed."

I don't. When death comes, I want to be stripped of any medically usable body parts, be wrapped in a quilt one of my black friends made for me, be put in my coffin and have the top nailed down with those square nails.

However, somebody will first have to take out the Rose Point Crystal, complete service for twelve including water pitcher and butter dish, that's stored in it. The crystal was a gift from an elderly relative, but I had no place to put it in my crowded cabinets, so it is stored in my coffin.

My grave marker won't be one of those fancy examples of the stonemason's art, nor will it have a flowery epitaph. I'd like to have some words from one of Jan Struther's poems:

> She was twice blessed:
> She was happy;
> She knew it.